DO NO HARM

BULLYING AND HARASSMENT IN THE NHS

DAVID MCCAFFREY

Britain's Next
BESTSELLER

To those who give their passion, dedication and resolve to care for others; without reward, without expectation.

FOREWORD

'Not supported in meetings… my career and promotional opportunities blocked.'

'I realised from the very start that no matter how distant my relationship with the doctors might become, I had to be most friendly with the nurses, if I was ever to get our health service going properly.' *Aneurin Bevan - 1946*

'Management questioned my need for counselling.'

'Were there none who were discontented with what they have, the world would never reach anything better.' *Florence Nightingale - 1887*

'I would try and engage and contribute to conversations, however I was not acknowledged. On several occasions when asking questions, she wouldn't even turn to face me. Being treated like this made me feel worthless and unimportant.'

'Not everyone has been a bully or the victim of bullies, but everyone has seen bullying, and seeing it, has responded to it by joining in or objecting, by laughing or keeping silent, by feeling disgusted or feeling interested.' *Octavia E. Butler - 1989*

'Management called me a 'stupid girl'. '

'We value every person – whether patient, their families or carers, or staff – as an individual, respect their aspirations and commitments in life, and seek to understand their priorities, needs, abilities and limits. We take what others have to say seriously. We are honest and open about our point of view and what we can and cannot do. ' *The NHS Constitution- 2015*

INTRODUCTION

Bullying is a very emotive word.

Say you don't like Susan who you work with, and no one pays much attention.

Say you hate Susan who you work with, and people's ears prick up.

Say Peter is being mean or picking on you, and people aren't particularly that engaged.

Say Peter is bullying you, and all of a sudden you have a great deal of attention being paid to your claims.

Remove the implied actions the word 'bully' conjures up, and you're left with a noun that means someone who is habitually cruel, overbearing, a thug, a pimp, intimidating... no matter which version of the dictionary you use, Oxford or online, that is pretty much how it is described.

What it doesn't tell you is that it is also an extremely subjective word. Just like the words happy, depressed and excited, bully doesn't mean the same thing to everyone.

I'll give you an example. Many years ago, I was fortunate enough to interview successfully for a new position. I was thrilled. More than thrilled; being advised I had got that particular job was one of the best moments of my life (up until that moment, I'd neither had children nor met George Lucas. I leave it to you to decide which one trumped the other!).

I was so excited.

On my first day, I was told two things -

1. "You weren't the first choice for the job, you know."
2. "We think the project you've been employed to roll out is a load of crap."

I HAVE PARAPHRASED, BUT THAT WAS GENERALLY THE GIST

Now, me being me, instead of being offended, I said to myself, "Now, self. Number one doesn't matter because you're here now; you got the job that you wanted - call it fate, call it luck, call it karma - but, you have it, so don't mess it up!"

I also took Number two as a challenge and said to myself, "Okay, I'm going to prove all you wrong."

And I did.

A year later, my colleague and I, who'd worked solidly on the project, won an audit award for our efforts.

But that was how I chose to handle it. Having been psychologically bullied by my father since being a child and physically bullied at school from the age of nine to sixteen, someone telling me those things didn't resonate with me in any way that I would have construed as bullying.

However, and this is where it becomes crucial and will define how you view what follows in this book, that was just my interpretation of the situation.

Someone else may have felt differently.

Was it bullying?

To me, bullying is a continuous wearing down and/or persecution of someone in a manner that makes them uncomfortable, upset or emotionally hurt.

According to Acas, bullying can be persistent or an isolated incident (Acas. Bullying and Harassment at Work: March 2015).

Also according to Acas, behaviour considered bullying by one person may be considered firm management by another (Acas. Bullying and Harassment: A guide for managers and employers: March 2014).

The familylives site, BullyingUK define bullying as repeated behaviour.

Already you have three sources which offer varying definitions of the word.

So as Shakespeare once said, therein lies the rub.

The purpose of this book is not to try and find a definitive answer to the 'what constitutes bullying' question; as mentioned, it is subjective, open to interpretation and often a personal perspective.

Instead, this book is going to try and demonstrate that, whether readers, chief executives and heads of service wish to believe it or not, bullying is a pernicious problem in the NHS.

Of course, it will be present elsewhere, in other organisations and establishments. I wish I could address their concerns too, but I can only speak of what I know and hope that, in some small way, perhaps what is told here may start a movement that will empower other employees to speak up if they feel they are being bullied at work.

This isn't only my opinion; otherwise, this book you hold in your hands would have little to no credibility.

This statement is backed up by many high profile and respected individuals.

Though this will be addressed throughout the course of the narrative, here are a few comments made in the last few years -

"Bullying is completely unacceptable and the ongoing work to tackle it is vital for all NHS organisations, leaders and staff."

Sue Covill, director of Development and Employment at NHS Employers. The Guardian, 2016

"We see the effects of these changes in the NHS: imposing a market ethos on health care staff, and a focus on indicators and targets, has led to the distortion of care... a narcissistic denial of reality deflects the citizens' attention from a much needed social critique. Understanding how narcissism underpins policy making, and how it becomes increasingly prevalent in social destructive ways of managing employees and manipulating the public, is there a necessary first step towards re-engaging with the political process."

Marianna Fotaki, Professor of Business Ethics. British Politics and Policy, 2018

"One thing that worries me more than anything else in the NHS is bullying... we're taking about something that is permeating the delivery of care in the NHS."

Sir Ian Kennedy. Bristol Royal Infirmary inquiry, 2009.

"I heard much evidence suggesting that members of staff lived in an atmosphere of fear of adverse repercussions in relation to a variety of events. Part of this fear was promoted by the managerial styles of some senior managers... A management style giving the appearance of bullying was not confined to director level. I heard evidence of a culture of bullying."

Robert Francis QC. Independent Inquiry into care provided by Mid Staffordshire NHS Foundation Trust January 2005 - March 2009 (Volume 1), 2010

"Not only is bullying widespread at every level, but there is some evidence that a particular type of 'corporate psychopath' may be responsible for a disproportionate amount of bullying."

Roger Kline. Bullying - the silent epidemic in the NHS, 2013

Throughout these pages, you will read many personal accounts from individuals who believe they have experienced bullying while working in and for the NHS. All trusts are anonymised, as are the individual's names. You may think some of the stories sound familiar, but that is most likely because you can, in some way shape or form, relate to what you are reading.

These reflections are the personal experiences of individuals; some are high-level management, some are nurses, some are occupational therapists, others are radiologists - all are courageous in sharing their stories.

I will present the facts as I know them.

I leave you, dear reader, to come to your conclusion as to what they show.

Ultimately, we are here to decide whether an organisation that dedicates itself to the care of others holds the same philosophy for staff.

The philosophy of Do No Harm.

ALICIA'S STORY

NHS EMPLOYEE

I have been nursing since I was 18 years old, having spent 30 years in the same organisation.

Nursing was my vocation and my life. There was nothing, outside of my family, I loved more.

I had been working in theatres, where I had been flourishing from a learning and enjoyment perspective when the opportunity arose for a sister's post.

I was fortunate enough to be successful in the interview for the position and felt everything was heading in the right direction. I could support my colleagues and help really drive the caring agenda forward.

My slightly older colleagues, who had been employed and working there longer than I, didn't necessarily agree and appeared to be threatened by my knowledge and enthusiasm.

My manager was of little help during this challenging period; being self-driven and not particularly a team player, I felt that I was unable to rely on her for support.

This challenging time culminated in me being accused of bullying by a staff nurse and healthcare assistant, both of whom I had known for some time.

It became clear that they were subtly attempting to influence other teams members by always chipping in with underhand comments and turning opinions against me.

It became clear that some staff nurses had some serious power when it came to decision making in the unit and only served to illustrate that I was not working in a democracy.

I was away on holiday when I received a letter from the trust containing the accusations of bullying along with additional accusations that concerned jokes made.

It was clear that what we know as 'office banter', something that a majority of staff members engage in, had been twisted into something a little more insidious.

A calm conversation I had held with a member of staff was turned into an accusation where I had been 'angry and aggressive'.

I challenged the accusations vehemently, at one point querying that if I had been so aggressive during a conversation on the unit, why had no one else heard or witnessed anything?

It was clear that my manager and the organisation had already formed an opinion and that nothing I said would be good enough to help them see what was happening - that colleagues, feeling threatened by the fact I am a good nurse, decided to manufacture stories that cast me as an erratic employee.

I made one of the saddest decisions of my life - I decided to leave rather than work another day in that organisation.

ONE

Randi Weingarten said you can't be against bullying without actually doing something about it.

I believe this to be true.

Addressing the issue isn't always as easy as that, and there is an excellent reason why.

It is a sociological phenomenon called diffusion of responsibility. You may have heard it called the Bystander Effect.

Picture this - you're walking along the street, and someone collapses just ahead of you. You're concerned, perhaps even worried, despite the fact this person is a total stranger.

You don't know them. You've never seen them before.

Moreover, you feel compelled to do something.

However, you also feel something else.

It's a similar feeling to embarrassment. It hasn't taken root entirely yet, after all, you haven't been

4

involved in a situation where you have a requirement to express shame.

But you might end up in such a scenario if you assist the gentleman or lady who has fallen in front of you.

What if they're drunk? What if it's some prank ala Beadle's About?

So what do you do?

You do absolutely nothing.

Now, there is a simple explanation for this. It's not because you're evil and have an innate desire to see someone suffer, or maybe even die. You are genuinely concerned about this person's wellbeing and want to know that they are okay, or at least going to be.

But still, you do nothing.

Because you assuage your risk of embarrassment and guilt for not intervening by assuming or reassuring yourself that the person behind you will do it instead.

Alex Lickerman (2010) put it like this. 'When a task is placed before a group of people, there's a strong tendency for each to assume someone else will take responsibility for it — so no one does.'

This is what happens in an environment where there are bullies present.

In the case of this book, the environment is the NHS.

The subject of bullying in the National Health Service has been raised countless times.

As recently as 2016, a survey conducted by The Guardian found that 86% of respondents thought that bullying was a big problem, while at least three-quarters felt the health service didn't take it seriously enough. Add some heavy hitters like Robert Francis QC noting in his Mid Staffordshire NHS Trust Public Enquiry report that there was a 'pervasive culture of fear in the NHS and certain elements of the Department of Health' and Sir Ian Kennedy saying in 2009 that he was worried more than anything else about 'the corrosive impact of bullying among NHS staff' and you cannot deny that it is a pernicious problem in, what is supposed to be, the most caring of organisations.

It is important to note that Robert Francis referred to bullying repeatedly throughout the Mid Staffordshire report, yet didn't make one recommendation about stopping it, nor did the Government in their response to the Francis Report.

One could argue that it was acknowledged it's prevalent, was summarily ignored and, is, therefore, condoned.

This is something we will touch upon in a later chapter.

However, first, an important question to ask is whether this phenomenon only applies to the NHS, to which the answer would be, of course, no.

First, explore why we have to look at the concept itself.

Bullying is nothing new, yet the meaning and interpretation of the word have changed drastically over the last 200 years.

In the early 18th century, the word was associated with physical or verbal harassment associated with death, isolation of extortion in children (Koo, 2007). What could now be termed as aggressive behaviour, was then seen as mischief, misadventure and a part of growing up.

The first recorded example of bullying was noted in The Times in 1862 when they ran a story concerning a soldier who had died due to bullying. His being subject to 'constant vexations and attack' was met with criticism at the time, as the behaviours that had led to his death were still seen as normal behaviour. However, The Times were defiant in their views and vocal about how specific actions could lead to harmful consequences.

Time moved on with change slow to catch up until Dan Olweus, a professor in Psychology, conducted his study on bullying amongst students using his personally developed research methods (Hazelden Foundation, 2007). His work not only expanded understanding of the word 'bully' but increased awareness and ultimately had a part to play in bringing enhanced guidelines concerning the protection of children into schools.

Sadly, we know this doesn't always hold.

The news is frequently littered with reports of children dying at the hands of individuals while at school, sometimes perpetrated by their classmates. The most distressing and infamous of these is the shooting at Columbine High School in 1999 when two teenage boys shot and killed many of their classmates after allegedly being bullied.

Add the advent of cyber-bullying into the mix not long after, and you have a world where you don't even have to be physically present to bully another individual - you can do it all from the safety and warmth of your own home or while riding on the bus.

So, where does this leave us with our beloved NHS?

It's important to state that, unequivocally, the National Health Service is our most precious and amazing social achievement. It's not the spontaneous, revolutionary provider of care that history would lead you to believe - the main catalysts for its creation being The Boar War, World War 1 and, to a lesser extent, World War 2.

Alongside Lloyd George's introduction of the National Health Insurance Act in 1919, the Beverage Report in 1942 and the election of Clement Attlee in 1945 which led to Aneurin Bevan being appointed Minister of Health, a National Health and Social Security Service was launched in 1948 on the back of these initiatives. This 'NHS' finally meant that 'the poor gained access to doctors and a range of treatments previously beyond their means, and no longer needed to worry economically about illness or injury.' (Why Was The NHS Created? 2013).

Alongside this groundbreaking, British institution, we were able to attract and recruit to it some of the greatest medical minds, nursing and doctor alike, from all across the world, a feat that continues even now.

There is nothing quite like it, anywhere.

And yet, this outstanding achievement has, over the course of decades, managed to achieve something altogether less inspiring and altogether more insidious.

A culture of bullying like no other.

We know it exists in other, if not the majority of, large businesses and organisations. How could it not? Anywhere that brings together a collection of individuals with different cultural beliefs, institutional expectations, social issues and inequalities, familiar histories and interesting personalities, is going to have a plethora of differing ideologies and viewpoints on life. This is only right and proper; however, you are also going to inherit multiple factors that can contribute to the complex issue of bullying behaviour.

However, this book is addressing the issue of this phenomenon within the health service, so this is where we shall be focusing our discussion, reflection and personal statements.

In 2015, The Telegraph published an article, 'Bullying in the NHS is getting worse, annual survey shows' that highlighted one in four NHS employees said they had suffered at the hands of managers and colleagues.

Add to that the earlier mention of Robert Francis and Ian Kennedy's beliefs and a pledge by ministers to tackle the 'cover-up culture', and you have to acknowledge the indisputable fact that bullying in the NHS is an insidious problem. One that only seems to be getting worse, if staff currently working in the health service are to be believed.

This book includes many personal statements from current and former NHS employees (names have been changed to protect their identities; locations, departments and hospitals have been omitted to protect those individuals) whose words and feelings have been collated in order for you to form your own opinion.

It is not the aim of this book to cast the entirety of the NHS in a bad light over bullying claims, but to highlight the fact that it is a behaviour which not only occurs but one that is denied in many circles and on many occasions.

This author believes every piece of reflection provided to be part of this book is not only a genuine experience but a courageous act of recall on the part of its writer. Dredging up bad and negative experiences can sometimes be just as traumatic as the experience itself.

One documented experience promoted many other healthcare workers to contact this author and volunteer to share their own stories of bullying to not only find some personal catharsis but to embrace the fact that it only takes one person to start a revolution. Once you have enough inertia and have reached a tipping point of people willing to speak up and out, you find that a subject will continue of its own volition.

The NHS has become the building blocks for a hierarchical structure that chooses to employ non-medical personnel into positions of power and suffer from their narcissistic attitudes and personalities.

Greek myth told of how the beautiful Narcissus died after falling in love with his image and, unable to leave this vision of beauty, lost his will to live.

It is the appointment of such individuals into executive positions that can be suspected as the root of many organisational bullying complaints and opinions.

Now, it must be said, as a society, we need the narcissist. It has its place in society, after all, who would be able to perform surgery if not the individual who can cut into flesh without freaking out - a surgeon must be devoid of empathy.

Narcissists are good news for companies because they dare to break new ground and push forward with their agendas on how things can be improved.

With it comes to a dangerous pervasiveness of

these narcissistic attitudes, one that slowly filters down to other individuals in positions of power who, through fear of being seen as less than competent or ineffectual, will adopt specific characteristics of this fixation of personal importance.

Such individuals will strive at any cost to achieve their goals, failing to learn from mistakes and assuming that by adopting the attitude of their superior, they will somehow be able to replicate their success.

Sadly, this is often not the case, and all that occurs is other individuals suffer.

Whenever perversion instrumentally overrides rationality - that is, whenever narcissism becomes dominant - other people grow to be seen as objects to be used (Fotaki, 2018).

In other words, if someone demonstrates bullying behaviour that seems to result in a success, others will be tempted to adopt the same approach in the hope of replication.

The above consideration is not only the opinion of this author; articles from Bristow (2015), Stern (2018), Ham (2012) and Maruthappu (2015) to name a few, all support this theory and some, its application to the NHS.

This bullying culture has risen most, in the opinion of this author, by others exerting undue pressure onto colleagues to get things done.

Healthcare workers wish to be seen as doing the very best that they can do. However, for some, this personally applied pressure can lead to a paranoid belief that when others do a good job, seemingly effortlessly, they are silently judged by others. If this relaxed approach to someone's work continues to result in positive outcomes without the need for applying pressuring techniques, some individuals feel they must resort to other methods to maintain their position of usefulness.

This is when, what could be perceived as bullying behaviour, comes into play.

References

Fotaki, M (2018) Narcissistic elites are undermining the institutions created to promote public interest. *British Politics and Policy.*

Hazelden Foundation, (2007). Olweus Bullying Prevention Program Research and History. *Retrieved from http://www.hazelden.org/web/go/olweus*

Koo, H. (2007). A Time Line of the Evolution of School Bullying in Differing Social Context. *Asia Pacific Education Review, Vol. 8, No. 1, 107-116.*

Lickerman, Al (2010) The Diffusion of Responsibility. *Psychology Today; Internet* November 2013. Why Was The NHS Created? *https://www.ukessays.com/essays/history/why-was-the-nhs-created-history-essay.php?vref=1* 9 *Accessed 28 May 2018)*

SUSAN'S STORY.

NHS EMPLOYEE

I started working at my trust in Autumn 2010.

It was my birthday and felt like one of the proudest days of my life. I had the job I had always dreamed of, and it felt amazing.

I initially started on a six-month contract; an agreement that was increased three times. Towards the end of my third extension, I was informed they could no longer keep me in the post. I was so upset and angry. I was rarely off sick and always tried to be accommodating to cover shifts when others were absent. It was difficult due to the fact I had small children, but I tried.

I decided that if I wanted to stay in the hospital, I had to fight, so I sent an email to the CEO who kindly replied and mentioned a job which had become available in one of the outpatient departments. It was suggested it would be great for me. I said I was interested of course. I jumped at the chance. I had an interview, and I got the job.

I was thrilled!

I heard through the grapevine that working in that department could be hard, but I decided I could deal with it. I finally had a permanent contract.

So, I started working there in December year or so later. The manager at the time was lovely - so supportive, understanding, kind and understood how hard things could be in that dept as she had dealt with it since she had started.

I would rely on her support and was so thankful for it.

Unfortunately, she decided she could no longer take working there and made the decision to leave.

I was crushed and terrified.

I was having problems by then with about five colleagues - two women I worked with on reception and some HCAs who decided to get themselves involved in bullying me. The two female colleagues had made it clear they didn't like me from the start. Apparently, they thought I was too posh and friendly and far too close to the boss, whom they had a dislike for.

Patients and other members of the staff liked me, and it became clear they could not cope with that. So, after a while, I felt I had to report my two colleagues for bullying me. I couldn't cope anymore. It was so hard to realise you have to do such a thing to your co-workers, but everything I did they criticised me for. They called me out in front of patients, joked about me, belittled me, made me look and feel stupid, made me feel ugly. Every look, word and smile I gave became harder and harder. I was being crushed inside, yet couldn't understand what I'd done to deserve this treatment. They supported each other in their campaign of harassment, but I had no one.

I was so alone.

I would cry before I came to work and would carry on crying when I left for the day. I would cry when with my children and with family. There is no other word to describe it other than horrific.

The group of them made my life very difficult, yet I foolishly hoped reporting them would make things better. What a huge mistake. It only got worse.

As one manager left, another was appointed. This could have been a great thing, but unfortunately, she was close friends with one of my persecutors and from the beginning, seemed to take an instant dislike to me.

She repeatedly told me that I was in the wrong job, asked if it was the place for me and advised that I should think about moving.

I cannot describe what it is like to have your manager and a senior member of staff, who should be leading by example, support the people who are bullying you.

I had suddenly been made to feel like a

trouble-causer while my manager became closer to my main abusers. One of them would tell me if I became upset that I was too sensitive and to not let things get to me.

"Try to let it go over your head," I would be told.

Instead of my concerns being investigated, I was told to ignore it.

I had panic attacks; the very thought of going to work filled me with dread.

One afternoon I was going to work I saw one of the union representatives. He stood and spoke to me while I cried, telling me that I needed to look after myself and take some time away. Maybe talk to my doctor.

I walked into work that afternoon and if looks could kill... I wanted to leave there and then. I had a panic attack at the thought of working between two women who ignored me, who only spoke and laughed to each other about me. I couldn't cope anymore.

My manager took me into the office, but it was so difficult to talk about it to her. She wasn't supportive or empathetic at all.

I eventually calmed down and went back to work, but the next day I took the union gentleman's advice and visited my doctor who advised that I should be off work for a while and that I should commence medication for my anxiety.

I spoke to some senior individuals and union personnel and told them I couldn't do it anymore; how much should one person have to cope with while at work.

I had tried so many times to help make things right with them, yet was stonewalled every step of the way. How could I be expected to work like that with no communication, all day every day?

Nine weeks in total. That's how long I was off work for. I didn't want to, but I had to take it - I just didn't feel well enough to go to back work.

I ended up having to wean off the tablets as they made me feel so tired, one of the more common side effects.

I genuinely believe that if it weren't for my children, I wouldn't be here today. Thinking of taking your own life only to get away from such pain is awful.

But I knew I had to carry on.

Before my return, I was told in a meeting that my main abuser and original instigator had chosen to retire.

I felt a strange mixture of relief and guilt, partly because I was told it had been motivated by my reporting her.

I was asked if I felt I could come back to work. I said I could but could I perhaps be sent to a different department.

I found out a job in rehabilitation had come up and hoped that if I went for an interview, I might get the job. So so, that's what happened, and it was all arranged.

Wow, my manager was not happy as, in her words, "There would be no one to cover the service."

She was desperate for me to stay, but I was

honest with her - why would I do that when I got zero support.

It turns out she was so unhappy about my decision and approval to work elsewhere that she spoke to my old boss. I had, by this time, explained my situation and acknowledged that I had been off on the sick for a protracted period, but that it was only because it was so demoralising and challenging to work there with certain people.

However, it was all for nothing. My manager interfered, and I didn't get the job.

I was scared. No, not scared - terrified. So many emotions flooded through me, knowing I'd have to go back to that place.

Something had happened that made my return slightly easier. They had employed a man in the department.

We hit it off, and I thank god for that. It was tinged with sadness as he ended up suffering at the hands of the same individual who had been bullying, me. Everything he did was criticised, he was belittled in front of others. God, it was so awful to see, but I was relieved it wasn't me. That is what they had done to me. Made me happy that someone else was suffering instead of me.

And on it went. I got so sick in meetings that my manager would just sit there, while I was berated and criticised, and say nothing. I would have to fight for myself every time, in every meeting, feeling my stomach flip with anxiety to the point I thought I was going to be sick.

I was determined I wasn't going to let that woman continue making me feel the way she did. Easier said than done.

The bullying continued until the day I was dismissed. I had been off work again because of what I was dealing with and was told I couldn't have any more time off.

I tried, I did, but being faced every day with the same humiliating and belittling behaviour that no one would attempt to stop was just too much. Moreover, to cap it all off, I was involved in a car crash! Thankfully it wasn't severe, but it was bad enough to write off my car.

I was in a hell of a state. I rang my manager the next day and told her what had happened. She advised that she expected me back given my sickness record. I felt ok, so agreed but wow, the next day I could hardly move. I had to tell her but thought 'it's only one day, then I'll be fine' so I went back the day after that. However, I was still in pain and couldn't move my neck. My walking wasn't good, but I was now too scared to be absent from work again.

I made it in, at which point one of the consultants asked me what I was doing there and why wasn't I resting at home? He said I had to look after myself and needed to go home or the consequences could be grave.

I took his advice, informed my manager and left, giving her all the ammunition she needed to get rid of me.

I stupidly thought that it wouldn't come to

that. I appreciated the sickness policy, but surely they would take into account that I had been in a car accident that wasn't my fault. On top of everything that had occurred, I was sure she wouldn't take it any further.

I was wrong again.

When I was off work, my Mam was so concerned that I would hurt myself she got a sick-note from my husband and, without my knowledge, took it into work. She was so upset about what was happening.

The senior member of staff she met with refused to speak to her but arranged for her colleague and a representative from H.R to talk with her.

The road to Hell, etc., etc., my manager didn't speak to me for up to six months upon my return, and when she did speak, it was filled with criticism. It even resorted to physical assault where she would pull my hair, saying "What the hell is that you have done to your face!" It got so bad, with her saying anything to belittle me that, in the end, I had to say something.

I went into the office with her and asked why she kept belittling me. She replied that the member of staff, who had left shortly after my joining, was like a mother to her and that she would never forgive me or forget what had happened. She stated that her going was basically all my fault.

I spoke to my manager about her comments. They did nothing

On my return to work, she took great pleasure in telling me I had been put on a stage three sickness report and had to attend a meeting. I was terrified but hoped I could find a way to get through it.

Weeks went by then, the actual week of the meeting, I got the pack that detailed everything my manager had said and thought about me.

There wasn't a single, positive thing written by her. It was all demoralising, heartbreaking and terrible.

I knew upon reading it that I was gone. Done. My dream job had been lost and taken away from me.

So, we got to January - I took a bag to work, spoke little to the people I had worked with, put my belongings in a bag and carried out my duties as always. I finished the day knowing I would never be seeing them again nor working there anymore.

The eventual meeting was held by people who didn't know me and didn't know what my manager and the others had put me through. Nor did they seem to be interested. They only appeared, when it was all completed, to have taken her word for it all. I tried to put my side across, but the decision had been made before I even got there.

After seven years of bullying me, she had finally won.

_____

TWO

'HE SPEAKS TO WHOEVER HE WANTS TO SPEAK
TO. IT MAKES PEOPLE FEEL EXCLUDED. HE
WOULDN'T DO THAT WITH ME, IT ALWAYS FELT
LIKE HE WANTED MY APPROVAL AND TO HAVE ME
ON HIS SIDE.'

The 2014 staff survey in England identified that the NHS exists on bullying the people who work in it (NHS, 2014), with 24% of staff reporting that they had experienced bullying, harassment or abuse either form their line manager or other colleagues. Within that number, 44% were reported incidents of bullying and harassment.

A subsequent survey in 2017 showed that the figure had remained static, with again, 24% of staff claiming reports of bullying. Additional research a year earlier by the University of Leicester (2016) demonstrated that 21% of mental health workers had reported being bullied, with a further 8% discriminated against by their managers.

What does this rudimentary example of data illustrated here demonstrate?

One could argue it suggests that, despite trusts having anti-bullying polices by any other name, they seem to not be robust enough to not only address actual incidents of bullying, but to help prevent them in the first place.

It is understandable that employees might feel that their maligned perceptions of distributive justice are accurate, when managers fail to execute the appropriate dignity at work policies following staff reports of violation.

Violation.

It's a strong word, something more appropriate when discussing physical assault. Yet bullying and harassment are indeed a violation - a violation of someone's sense of self and appreciation.

Consider the below from a senior individual currently working in the NHS:

"I felt I was being forced into taking on too much; major additions were being made to my role without proper consultation. It was unclear who was making actual work-based decisions about how we, as a team, were supposed to function. But when you ask, you get no answers. I was told to 'tow the line'.

"I was asked to provide a reply to an e mail regarding issues within a service I manage. I felt it was appropriate to answer truthfully, however following my reply to a senior member of the organisation, I was asked why I had answered the email truthfully during a meeting with my manager.

"I have just begun to feel as though the NHS has become this corporate machine, a place where you are being forced or coerced into behaving a certain way. It got to the point where I felt I could no longer be there until I got my head straight about what I wanted for my future career... about whether I was prepared to move on or conform, and become the employee they wish me to be, someone who could 'tow the line'.

"I ended up going off on the sick. My most recent conversation involved a statement that went along the lines of 'If your sick note is longer than a week, then your role may be modified without your involvement."

Once again, we are entering into a complicated area, that which includes the aforementioned personal perception.

Bullying often has, at its core, multiple causes relating to an individual, group or an organisation. A paper published in 2013 by the National Institute for Health Research (Illing, Carter, Thompson *et al*) stated that men engaged in workplace aggression more than women, citing actual leadership styles as a potential cause. Yet Psychologies (2010) identified that it was female colleagues that needed to be observed, particularly regarding their behaviour towards men.

A classic Seinfeld episode had George and Jerry discussing 'wedgies' and how boys encourage each other to get physical. When Jerry asks Elaine if girls do things like that, she responds by saying, 'Oh, no. We just tease each other until one of us develops an eating disorder.'

Amusing in the context of the show, indeed. But

there is a great deal of truth to such a statement if other women are to be believed.

An anonymous source stated that 'women love to see men destroyed, but not other women, unless it's someone other than them doing it.'

These statements are supported by other high profile and inspirational women, figures such as Cheryl Dellasega, a relation aggression expert and author of six books; When Nurses Hurt Nurses, Mean Girls Grown Up, Girl Wars and Toxic Nursing to name a few.

Cheryl says that 'there are far more arenas for women to be openly competitive, but I don't think we've learnt to do it very well… instead of owning up to our desire to dominate… we prefer to release our feelings of envy and jealousy in more underhand ways. There are no closer relationships than between two women; we nurture, we care and we can read body language better than men - all of that can be used against someone when we're feeling insecure and is the tool that women use to destroy that relationship.'

Adjectives to describe female bullying include covert, subtle and manipulative.

Dellasega is further supported in an article by Ruchika Tulshyan (2012) who states that women can be nastier bullies than men, especially in the workplace for the theorised reason that history and inequality have unfairly denied women the chance to be considered equal to their male counterparts. For this reason, women have perhaps had to resort to drastic measures to secure positions of power or seniority; the downside being that there is less experience in this 'competitive' environment than amongst men.

That said, particularly in the NHS, the common perpetrators of bullying are managers, noted by Hoel and Cooper (2000) as often being tolerant of negative behaviours. Though the proportion of this group were identified as male, it is important to note that as males are overrepresented in managerial positions, this could account for the larger number of male perpetrators.

Now, the purpose of this book is not to cast any gender into disrepute; already we have read how men and women can be as bad as each other. It is their motivations behind such behaviour which are interesting.

Men seem to be ego-driven in regards to bullying-type behaviour, whereas women seem to use more indirect tactics and behave proactively in order to sabotage another colleagues career.

This theory is supported by Ruchika Tulshyan (2012) who wrote in Forbes that girls are taught to be critical about each other from adolescence, something that only becomes more vicious once they are in employment, particularly if it is a male-dominated environment.

However, the most important aspect to take away from this chapter is that bullying, in whatever shape or form, direct or indirect, subtle or overt, is abuse through the misuse of power and is something alive and well in the NHS. In fact, it could be argued that it is an integral part of NHS culture and that it would not exist in its current shape or form if not for bullying.

Now, it needs to be emphasised once again and will be throughout this book, that the NHS is an inspired organisation, frequently declared the best healthcare system in the world. When you compare it to the US, which is often declared the worst, denying care to many patients simply because they do not have health insurance, then we have something to always be proud of.

Efficiency, quality, access, provision of safe, co-ordinated and patient-centred care were all found by the Commonwealth Fund study in 2016 (Osborn, Squires, Doty *et al*) to be indicative of our NHS.

The only black mark reported against it was its poor record for keeping patients alive, as in, if the care had been provided in a timely fashion, they may not have died.

The issue of staff behaviour was not addressed in the Commonwealth survey, but one doesn't have to look far to see reports from current and former NHS employees that support the allegations of bullying and harassment.

Dr Kevin Beatt was a Cardiologist for nearly 30 years at Croydon NHS Trust before he was fired for being a whistleblower following concerns raised by him in regards to the treatment of patients and the dishonesty of senior management.

Despite the seemingly bottomless resources of the NHS when it comes to protecting themselves against allegations, Dr Beatt fought them in multiple, financially draining appeals to have his whistle-blowing actions supported and, in a cruel irony, be also acknowledged by an Employment Tribunal that he was fired for the same reason.

He now has a fund raising page to help support his legal fees whilst he continues his battle to have

Croydon NHS Trust acknowledge that he followed the whistleblowing policy and to also provide him with compensation; money he is owed to the fact that the trust were found guilty of his unfair dismissal.

The trust were accused of being 'vague and unconvincing, 'unreliable', inconsistent' and providing evidence to convey a 'false impression.'

They gave a counter-statement that he had been dismissed for making 'unsubstantiated and unproven allegations of an unsafe service' and appealed the decision.

The message behind his crusade only serves to clarify the points raised so far and those that will be shared throughout this book - that individuals have to stand up and be counted, whatever the personal cost, if the NHS is to survive because staff must be allowed to properly raise concerns without fear of retribution.

The subsequent pieces of reflection from staff working and previously employed by the NHS will provide you with a clear picture of the types of behaviours that take place every day.

References

2016 Commonwealth Fund International Health Policy Survey *(Robin Osborn, David Squires, Michelle M. Doty, Dana O. Sarnak, and Eric C. Schneider, M.D.)*

Illing JC, Carter M, Thompson NJ, Crampton PES,

Morrow GM, Howse JH, *et al.* Evidence synthesis on the occurrence, causes, consequences, prevention and management of bullying and harassing behaviours to inform decision making in the NHS. *Final report. NIHR Service Delivery and Organisation programme; 2013.*

Hoel H, Cooper CL. Destructive Conflict and Bullying at Work, Manchester School of Management, University of Manchester Institute of Science and Technology. *Report for British Occupational Health Research Foundation (BOHRF), 2000.*

Tulshyan, R (2012) Why Women are the worst kind of bullies. *Forbes.*

ABIGAIL'S STORY

NHS EMPLOYEE

Having over thirty years of nursing experience and a variety of senior lead roles, I had developed substantial leadership, management, service improvement and facilitation skills.

My experiences provided me the opportunity to challenge practice; inspire; motivate and empower others to pioneer and champion others to push for improvements in clinical practice, quality and service development.

I considered myself to be very much a team player and actively encouraged colleagues, at all levels, to take a more active role in multidisciplinary working.

I cared passionately about the quality of care patients received, which I believe was reflected in my dynamic approach to practice development and service improvement.

My work meant everything to me.

I was promoted to a new senior clinical role, Nurse Consultant, and over the following five years, went on to develop the role and the service as part of the Specialist Nursing Team.

Unfortunately the role was put at risk in 2006 due to financial constraints the trust was experiencing. Through the process of redeployment, I was invited to continue to support the service in my previous role as a Clinical Nurse Specialist. So, for a further two years I continued to lead the specialist nurse service, ran my nurse-led clinics and managed the budget.

And then, one day, I collapsed at work.

Too upset to continue my shift, I was sent home by the Clinical Matron. The trigger for my distressed state being that, having returned from a busy nurse-led clinic, a colleague had decided to take "time owing" and had gone home without discussion and with no thought to the remainder of outstanding tasks for that day.

I was mentally and physically exhausted which led to a long period of sickness. I was later diagnosed with reactive depression.

Of course, something like this doesn't happen overnight. This wasn't a case of 'having a bad day'. There were long-standing, contributory factors.

These included, but weren't exclusive to -

- My job as Nurse Consultant was put at risk not once, but twice, which led to a long drawn out process; a process not handled very well by management and the Senior Nurse.
- Poor team dynamics both within the specialist nursing team and medical team.
- Poor communication within the team.
- Two work colleagues had a very different work ethic regularly taking "time owing" at short notice without consultation.
- Jealously and resentment between team members.
- Not being involved in team discussions and the decision-making process despite being responsible for certain aspects of the service, leading to feelings of frustration and isolation.
- Decisions made with external partners without my knowledge or involvement despite being the lead and my responsibility. This resulted in being made to look foolish on a number of occasions leading to feeling of low self-esteem and self-worth.
- Despite being a nursing lead for the service, a junior colleague, who had previously left the trust, was still in correspondence with some members of the nursing team and one

of the consultants. She was better informed than I regarding service changes or developments.

All of these issues and more, were highlighted with the Senior Nurse on several occasions, yet no action was taken.

The list goes on and sadly, on. I was often excluded from team meetings, discussions and social activities, all of which contributed to my feeling of isolation. The details of these issues are too many to share; the toll they would take great.

There are also other issues which I feel it is inappropriate to mention. It was only through counselling that I came to realise that many of the behaviours shown towards me were actually bullying in nature. At the time you don't even realise the extent to which they are affecting you.

But it did affect me. How?

- I felt traumatised
- Broken/Damaged
- Low self-esteem and self-worth
- Emotional
- Angry
- Physically sick every time I thought of work
- Felt physically sick if the phone rang
- Feeling as though boiling hot water was being poured over me

- I couldn't attend formal meetings on site and had to have home visits from the occupational health nurse
- Couldn't cope with seeing anyone from work, even close friends
- Withdrew myself from contact with other work colleagues
- Didn`t trust immediate work colleagues, some medical and senior management
- Low mood, lacked tolerance and I also became irritable and short tempered
- Didn't want to be in company of others, even close friends and family
- Went grocery shopping late evening so as to avoid being in large groups of people
- Poor appetite, weight loss, poor sleeping pattern
- Negative attitude, unable to think positively or make plans about the future.

And so, my life went on hold for a period of six months. Though this time and with the support of my GP, a counsellor and Occupational Heath Doctor I was able to return to working in the trust. And that would, should have been wonderful. Unfortunately I was unable to return to the role I loved and a service that I had helped to develop, as I didn't want to put my health at risk again.

I met with the nursing director who arranged for me to join her team to help deliver a national service improvement initiative. This opportunity helped me to further develop my knowledge and skills and improve services across the Trust.

The programme of work was very successful, winning national awards for the trust. In doing so, I was also given the opportunity to once again feel as though I was "making a difference" to patient care.

On reflection, this core value that has always driven me in my life and work, had been restored. In turn, I was able to heal, regain my self-worth and feel whole again.

I hope sharing my experience will go some way to raising awareness of how, despite being a caring organisation, we fall short of caring for each other.

People, staff, colleagues, friends, call them what you will, are any organisation's biggest asset and biggest resource, thereby making awareness of these issues essential. Nowhere is this more pertinent than the NHS, an organisation that prides itself on caring and compassion.

It is this compassion and care that must extended to everyone in the organisation if it is to remain healthy.

THREE

'HE WOULDN'T ALWAYS ADHERE TO RULES AND
REGULATIONS, BUT WAS ALLOWED TO GET AWAY
WITH IT.'

Once I mentioned I was writing a book on bullying and harassment in the NHS, I expected... hoped actually... to be told that the story I had shared on my blog was crap and that I was really the only one who had an issue with the behaviours towards colleagues in the National Health Service.

It was both humbling and heartbreaking to find myself inundated with messages (not being one for hyperbole, I literally mean I received more than a 100 messages from NHS employees, local and national (some international), asking if they could share their experiences of bullying with me).

The interesting thing about such a response is that I was once told that one particular organisation did not have a problem with bullying, yet more than 70 of these messages (more since this book was published), are from this particular trust.

From this, you can infer two things.

- They are genuinely not aware that such behaviour exists
- They are aware and choose to do nothing about it

Upon reading those points, you will have already come to the conclusion that neither is acceptable.

If a trust were to not be aware bullying and harassment exists in their organisation, one could argue that they are detached from their staff and have little actual interaction with them on a regular basis to know whether or not they are happy at work. This could be extended to SDRs (Staff Development Reviews), one-on-one meetings and even huddles or ordinary catch ups.

The fact that any NHS organisation would have this opinion is in direct contradiction to the 2017 NHS Staff Survey (NHS Staff Surveys online) which found that bullying and harassment remain an extensive problem in the health sector, with one in four people having reported that they have experienced bullying in some way.

When further results analysed show that NHS employees (medical and nursing) stated they have suffered psychological stress due to bullying, and you have a compelling argument for the fact that is does and has taken place for a long period of time, with reports going back as far as Roger Kline's report on bullying in the NHS published in 2013.

Indeed, most recently in 2017, The Guardian published an article 'Bullying and being bullied is everywhere now, at every level in the NHS' (the guardian.com accessed 25/08/2018) which dealt with the issue amongst the medical profession, particularly surgeons.

Judy Evans, a consultant plastic surgeon at a private Nuffield hospital said that, "What can be perceived as harmless banter... can actually be deeply offensive, or even abusive. It can be incredibly subtle but terribly destructive... I know of surgeons who have considered taking their own lives, others who have left the professions because of bullying surgeons' bad practice going unchallenged."

The incidences of doctors and consultants suffering from bullying, to the extent that it becomes the cause of mental health issues, may be viewed as surprising, particularly as medical staff are considered to be made of a particular brand of individual. By that I mean that, a consultant surgeon for example, has to inherently have certain psychological traits in order to cut into someone's flesh and not be emotionally effected by it.

It wouldn't do to have Mr. Baker, vascular surgeon, performing a carotid endarterectomy and becoming emotionally unhinged whilst John Smith's neck is open wide. Such professionals in the health service are seen as being made of sturdier stuff, some even viewed as almost messianic.

To learn that such a mentally strong individual can be broken down psychologically, piece by piece, by another's words, goes to show how true devastating and permeating bullying behaviour can truly be.

PETER'S STORY

PHYSIOTHERAPIST NHS

I am 59 years old and have worked in health care for 33 years, 28 of which were in the NHS.

I joined a trust in 2002. Exciting times, new experiences, fresh location.

I was bullied from the day I began to the day I retired in November 2013.

On my first day, my manager said that I wasn't welcome in her department and that I should consider working somewhere else.

That was my first day.

I, of course, had never met her before so was shocked by her attitude. The next manager above her wasn't having any of it and insisted I worked in her department.

She reluctantly agreed, but refused to provide any clerical or management support. I had to do my own administration, post out appointments to patients and deal with telephone enquiries, all whilst still being expected to carry a full caseload.

None of the other staff were expected to work with the same level of expectation.

Skip to 2008, I was accused of lying down on a plinth during my lunch breaks.

I used to eat a sandwich and read.

Relaxed? Certainly.

Worthy of scrutiny? Unlikely.

Nevertheless I was secretly photographed and the Head of Service dragged me over the coals for lying down during my lunch break. He also came up with a vague accusation of bullying but refused to provide me with any details.

I suspect he had found out that I was openly critical of his management style after he had undermined my specialist service and thus had developed a vendetta against me.

In 2010, my manager, together with one of her colleagues, wrote a letter of complaint about me to the Head of the Service. I don't know the contents of the letter, but I think it implied that I was bullying her, not the other way round.

The Head of Service ordered an investigation and warned that the result could mean me being dismissed from the Health Board (which it had now become).

The investigation took 18 months and was carried out by a manager from a different service in the interests of parity.

When the report came out, I was exonerated whilst it was highly critical of my manager. Yet I received a formal warning, apparently on account that I had made an administration error.

In my opinion and from my experience, the Head of Service was a narcissistic bully who colluded with my manager. I am convinced that this individual had persuaded my manager to write that letter of complaint against me, although I have no proof.

Even after I had been exonerated, the Head of Service continued to bully me until I had had enough and retired in 2013.

I think he was frustrated that the investigation didn't go the way he wanted it to.

Yet, the worst thing throughout all of it was the way my union representation colluded with the Head of Service. Psychologically, I think they did more harm than the actual Head of Service.

That is my story.

I still get upset thinking about it all. It all just brings back such painful memories.

FOUR

'AFTER HE RETURNED FROM THE RECENT
SICKNESS ABSENCE EPISODE, HE SPOKE TO THE
WHOLE TEAM AND SHARED WITH US THAT HE
WAS SO ILL HE WAS NEARLY ADMITTED TO A
MENTAL HEALTH FACILITY. I WAS SHOCKED BY
THIS STATEMENT AND BELIEVED IT TO BE
UNPROFESSIONAL.'

Bullying isn't necessarily a behavioural trait that inherently exists in someone's character.

On the contrary and certainly based upon my own experiences, individuals who I would never have seen as bullies nor who had ever displayed such traits, became tacit examples of such a behaviour.

But why?

The Quine Workplace Bullying questionnaire conducted by Northumbria University as part of their final report for NHS employers in 2016 (Workplace bullying: measures and metrics to use in the NHS, Illing *et al*, 2016) identified that low levels of job satisfaction and high levels of job-induced stress were just a few of those circumstances that appeared to coincide with bullying in the workplace.

Results suggested that 'the provision of a

supportive positive work environment may help to protect people's health and wellbeing.' (Illing *et al*, 2016)

Indeed, the aforementioned factors were supported by Burnes and Pope (2007) who highlighted that of all public sector workplaces, the NHS was prone to more negative behaviour than others. Factors such as low job mobility were mentioned (Zapf *et al*, 2003), with Leymann (1996) stating that the bureaucratic and impersonal nature of public sectors organisations, coupled with the low priority traditionally given to management skills, an authoritarian management style adopted by the NHS, frequent organisational change, impossibly tight deadlines and targets and aggressive behaviour as a deliberate management tactic all contributed to a smelting pot of circumstances that are ideal for nurturing bullying behaviour and, most importantly, force those who have difficulty coping in such environments to adopt behaviours alien to their character.

Interestingly, though unsurprisingly, defining the concept of bullying with any degree of accuracy has proven historically difficult. Touched upon in an earlier chapter, we can add to the notion of bullying as one that involves, but is not exclusive to, incivility, mobbing and victimisation. Pearson *et al* (2001) found that one of the most destructive factors, but a lesser form of workplace bullying was that of incivility.

Incivility is seen as a low intensity form of deviant behaviour with an ambiguous intent towards a particular individual but using vectors such as rude, insensitive or disrespectful behaviour towards others with an unclear intent to harm.

However, such an explanation is where the

concept of bullying can become blurred, as what is perceived by one as 'incivility' could be seen by anywhere as the aforementioned 'work place banter.'

A personal example I can draw upon is that of a comment I made once to a work colleague and personal friend of more than ten years.

This colleague was someone with who I associated with outside of work, so I do consider her a friend as opposed to a work colleague (indeed, this individual was one of the few people to stand by me during my own traumatic experiences with bullying and remains my friend to this day).

When my colleague arrived at work, her hair was windswept. Being the sarcastic dick that I am, I asked whether she had come into work on a motorbike… without a helmet.

She laughed, others laughed and she called me a knob. That was it and we remain friends to this day.

This comment was raised by someone else many years later with the twist that I was rude, had offended my colleague and that I was always inappropriate.

To those of you reading this book who don't know me, I would never attempt to convince you that I am not those things; that would be slightly self-servicing. However, those who do know me know that this was simply banter and me being (or thinking I was!) amusing.

The recipient of my quip was horrified that she had been used to try and illustrate an offence being caused where one didn't exist between her and I.

And so we come around in a full circle to the question of whether my comment was incivility, intended to be rude and destructive, or simply banter between friends?

References

Pearson, C.M., Andersson, L.M. and Wegner, J.W. (2001), "When workers flout convention: a study of workplace incivility." *Human Relations*, Vol. 54 No. 11, pp. 1387-419

Zapf, D., Einarsen, S., Hoel, H. and Vartia, M. (2003), "Empirical findings on bullying", in Einarsen, S., Hoel, H., Zapf, D. and Cooper, C.L. (Eds), *Bullying and Emotional Abuse in the Workplace, International Perspectives in Research and Practice, Taylor & Francis, London.*

DIANA'S STORY

NHS EMPLOYEE

This recollection begins about ten – fifteen years ago following an accident when I'd slipped on a wet floor in a social club - no alcohol involved.

I tore the ligament in my left knee and was off work for nearly a year following surgery, physiotherapy, splints etc. Given the circumstances, things went pretty smoothly until I found, following an MRI scan, out that I had Osteoarthritis in most of my joints.

I was only in my 30s.

I returned to work and things continued as normal, but every now and then one or two of my joints would become painful and swell as they had before I fell. Numerous times I went to the GP, only to be told take anti-inflammatories and that it was all because of the OA.

During this time if I got a cold, it would

really floor me and more often than not would turn into a chest infection. I was ward based then and the sickness absence policy was different.

After leaving an acute hospital, I joined the community and things became worse, although not in the beginning.

I became part of a team and I felt great for some time before my joints started acting up again. I was given anti-inflammatories again and told I had OA – again. However, this time around my fingers had started to alter, I had thickening of my knuckles and finger joints and my hands were painful and stiff, especially on a morning.

So, alongside the above, I was also sick due to musculoskeletal problems and several times ended up reaching stage 2/3 sickness/absence as I required two further surgeries to my left knee to trim cartilage following the earlier surgery.

All in all, I felt pretty lousy, but during this time I also felt supported as the clinical lead was great. I also had good support from the Occupational Health department.

Around this time, a move occurred in the district nursing service and I was moved to another location.

For the next couple of years I felt OK, but was still having joint problems, especially in my hands and feet. Then, out of the blue, I developed bilateral carpal tunnel. I woke up on this particular morning feeling like I'd slept on my right hand all night - I had no feeling; it was completely numb.

I went to work but, a few hours later, the numbness still hadn't wore off and the pain had gotten worse. I was sent home and went to the doctor's where I was given a sick note and was referred for possible surgery.

In total, I was off sick for four months because I required surgery on both hands, but separately. During this time, I was repeatedly asked if I would contemplate returning to work and being office based - light duties, that sort of thing.

It took me all my time to dress myself and do everyday activities because both of my hands were now totally numb, at least prior to the surgery. So, being asked to return to work felt a little like pressure.

I spoke to the doctor in Occupational Health and asked him what he thought; his response was definitely not because I would be unsafe. This was a response that my manager was unimpressed with, prompting her being abrupt over the phone and making me feel like I was being awkward.

That aside, I had the surgery, returned to

work and things ran fairly smoothly for a while. I had pain and some discomfort in one joint or another, but otherwise everything was going well.

Until it all really started.

About five or six years ago, I was off work more than I was at work. In one year, I had four different infections!

During this time I returned to work, feeling ill, but you don't want to let your colleagues down. Plus I felt pressured by my manager who, at the time, didn't appear to be concerned about me as an individual but more about her sickness figures.

When I had the Labyrinthitis, and whilst being as dizzy as a kipper, I was asked if I could return to work and triage for the team. It would be office-based and, despite being hardly able to hold my head up without feeling sick, I was assured by my Clinical Lead I would feel better when the the medication I had been commenced on was in my system. I was to be contacted at the end of the week and that was that.

During this time, my G.P had given me a sick note for two weeks and said she wanted to review me, but I returned to work as agreed, mostly because I felt pressured by my manager…. I lasted four hours.

The computer made me feel dizzy and I didn't want to leave, having only just arrived, but I just didn't feel well enough to work.

I was advised by my manager that I would trigger another episode of sickness because I'd returned to work, but I felt so ill it was the last thing on my mind.

Throughout these episodes of sickness, HR had become heavily involved. I'd began to feel like a squatter in Occupational Health.

I had several return to work interviews, told my manager that I felt unfairly treated and pressured to work due to staffing shortages. Whether this struck a chord I don't know, but the episode was only counted as continual. I was happy with the outcome.

And then things became worse.

Long story short, I suffered a work place injury. The locality manager, although giving a small laugh when she said it, basically said, "There's nothing that you could have possibly tripped on. Did you throw yourself on the ground on purpose?"

I'm paraphrasing, but that was the gist.

Why the hell would I do that?

I was again sent to Occupational Health and was again advised not to return to work, even on amended duties and office-based, as I wasn't insured.

This angered my manager who said Occupational Health were only there for guidance and I should be able to return (I had also twisted my ankle when I fell and much later found out, through ultrasound, I had fractured it and avulsed the tendon).

Couldn't make it up, right?

And because of all of this, I'd triggered level 3 sickness… again!

I ended up returning to clinical duties, with lots of discomfort in my ankle, but worked through it, afraid to be off anymore.

By this time, I'd received letters saying if I was off sick again my contract could be terminated.

Some days I felt so sore and ill I actually cried before going to work, but when at work you apply your laughing cheery face and get on with it.

I was stressed and not in a good place mentally. I developed shingles (again) on the right side of my face which extended from my scalp down to my chin.

I went to the GP who gave me meds and a sick note for two weeks with advice for me to be reviewed after.

As you can imagine, my manager wasn't happy at all.

I was asked if I could return to office duties again, but apply dressings to my face and wear a catering cap to cover my scalp. The thought of wearing this made me upset and very uncomfortable – I would have to walk in full view of patients on the floor below if I wanted to go to the toilet.

I mentioned this to my manager and was told, "Well, in that case, you can work office-based at another location."

I explained about the pain I had in my face and eye and was advised by my manager to take analgesia which I was taking already. Because of this face and eye pain, I again sought advice from Occupational Health who said there was no way I could work, so I was off sick, yet again.

By this time, I had triggered level 4 sickness.

Whilst awaiting my formal meeting for this situation, I was making a coffee at home when I dropped the kettle of boiling water over my left hand - the pain was excruciating to say the least.

I rang work and told my manager I was having to go to A&E and why.

My manager's response was, "Not again!"

I was then asked if I could just put a dressing on and come back to work?

I had no skin on the back of my left hand and down my fingers, so I advised that it wouldn't be possible. I even took photos in A&E to show how bad the injury was.

I returned to work after a couple of days, requiring twice weekly dressings at the surgery. Because my surgery opened and closed during the time I was working, I had to use holidays to cover my appointments.

When I showed my manager the photos

upon my return, she was aghast and seemed shocked at the extent of the injury. I later learned from other colleagues in the office that when she had learned of my situation, she had told them I had phoned in sick with a blister.

Upon finding this out, I felt so belittled.

During all of this, I had attended my GP regarding infection concerns and about the pain and swelling I had in my joints, especially my hands and feet. I was advised it was all related to my O.A.

I have to mention that, throughout all of this, I did have fantastic support from the RCN.

Once again, I returned to work, office-based as instructed by Occupational Health, and had my Formal Sickness/ Absence meeting.

In attendance were my union representation, the locality manager and her deputy. If I'm honest, they were very abrupt and devoid of any compassion which was unexpected given it was HR who had brought the case against me.

I was asked why was I accruing so much sick time, that my colleagues weren't and why wasn't I improving my sickness/absence? Why did I have a fall when no-one else had ever fallen in that location, it must have been fresh air that I tripped over... this was the kind of tone and theme of the entire meeting.

I explained what the GP had advised and was told that it was, "No answer."

In this meeting, HR dragged up my entire working career sickness record - all 25 years.

I felt like I was on trial and being totally disbelieved. I had letters from my GP, character references but it was all skimmed over.

I was asked whether I could guarantee I wouldn't be off again for at least two years.

I didn't say it out loud, but who could honestly give that guarantee?

My answer was, "I don't think I could give you a definite guarantee, but I will do anything and try my hardest to maintain my attendance."

This wasn't what they wanted to hear.

When myself and my union representation returned to the panel, I was told my contract had been terminated and that I had to work a 12 week notice.

I asked why I was being let go and was told that it wasn't because of my work and performance - they weren't in question - but that it was because of sickness.

I felt destroyed.

Returning to work for those 12 weeks was the hardest thing I had ever done. I was tearful, quiet, stressed and so angry.

I thought long and hard, but decided to appeal.

I went to my GP (who was, incidentally, shocked at the outcome of the meeting) and was referred to see a specialist.

I had been asking for this for some time and am uncertain whether my dismissal precipitated the decision. Whatever the reason, I was pleased.

I saw a lovely consultant, who was astounded I hadn't been referred years ago. In fact, it would be fair to say he was annoyed to the point he wrote his feelings in a letter to my G.P.

I had an ultrasound on each joint and emergency bloods taken. Not only did I have O.A confirmed, but I was diagnosed with Psoriatic Arthritis with a degree of Rheumatoid.

Basically, my immune system was in my boots because of the arthritis which was also the reason I'd developed carpal tunnel and had an intermittent 'flop' of my right foot. Turns out, the dropping of the kettle was due to weakened joints.

I was started on medication immediately and had to have injections every two weeks for three months.

The hospital doctor contacted Occupational Health and, with letters from both them and my union representative, I attended my appeal hearing regarding my dismissal.

Now, I have to give credit to the managers who sat on the panel, because they were absolutely lovely.

As soon as they were told there was evidence I had a long term condition that had affected my immunity, the decision was overturned and I was reinstated with the caveat that I wasn't clinical and I remained office based until I could be redeployed.

So, I returned to work and had a further meeting with a senior manager who was very abrupt in telling me that if a suitable position didn't appear, I would be put on the 12 week at risk register and, at any time, without warning, my contract could be terminated.

I have a suspicion that it suited management not to have a clinical nurse doing triage, therefore they allowed me to remain in the role for three years. Every day of those three years I thought would be my last day. In the end, it is only my opinion, but to be honest I was grateful. I needed the wage.

Health-wise, my medications were working great - odd flare up - but overall, I felt much better. That was until I was working one day when I suddenly felt like a baseball bat had hit me in the back and front of my head at the same time. It was so bad, I even cried out; my vision blurred and I vomited.

My line manager was there at the time and didn't appear overly concerned until one of the sisters, who had worked in neurology, voiced her concerns that I looked so ill.

I was allowed to go home an hour early.

I felt ill all night, with a blinding headache and nausea but I had a hospital appointment the following day so I thought I would mention it then.

My blood pressure was 210/130, high by anyone's standards, and I was seen by a different rheumatologist who advised me to see my GP, ASAP.

I duly followed his advice and was subsequently admitted to hospital with a suspected subarachnoid haemorrhage.

After a clear Lumbar puncture, I was diagnosed with Neuralgia and migraines.

My manager rang me the following day and said she'd rung to see how I was, but somehow managed to slip into the conversation, "When did I expect to be back?"

Because of all of the above situation, my arthritis medications were stopped in event they were the cause, but this in turn caused a major flare up all down my right side.

So, I was off sick again.

My manager rang me constantly to check how I was, but always asked when would I be back and didn't I think I could manage even a few hours on triage?

I felt low and under pressure to return to work and so very ill, I just didn't know what to think or where to turn.

I went to a different GP and broke down, crying in front of her. She was so supportive and said she thought I was suffering from depression. I was commenced on antidepressants.

Because of my impaired immunity and all the other things, I decided to apply for ill health retirement following several meetings with HR and my manager.

I was asked constantly when would I be returning to work, but I only felt they weren't interested in me as a person, just the service.

During all of this, my Mum, who lived with me, became very unwell and it was only last year that she had to go into residential placement.

To sum it all up, throughout all my sickness episodes I felt bullied into returning to work too early. Perhaps if I had taken long off work, I wouldn't have accrued as much sick leave as I did. Who knows?

My view is that the caring profession doesn't exist for the staff; they are a number that the management can bend and make perform at will. We are but puppets; they apply pressure and we conform.

Yes, of course there is a service to provide and run, with patients at the end of it who need our care.

But we, the carers and deliverers of that service, need care too. We need to know we are appreciated and looked after and not a disposable commodity. Otherwise, we become the very people that we are supposed to be providing care for.

Patients.

FIVE

"I DON'T THINK IT WAS ANY DIFFERENT BUT I'M NOT HERE ALL THE TIME. WHEN HE RETURNED HE SAID TO ALL OF US AS A TEAM WHY HE WAS OFF SICK. I THOUGHT IT WAS BRAVE AS HE DIDN'T HAVE TO DO IT."

Already, by this point in the book, it is clear that it is hard to credit an organisation whose primary focus to be the care of the sick, vulnerable and disabled, to have a terrible reputation for bullying and harassment.

A bizarre counterpoint for such a place of work is the supermarket chain, Asda (Glassdoor; accessed 23/9/2018). Workers there reported in an annual retail survey a sense of pride about their work, citing great staff to work with, good bonuses and nice working hours.

B&Q highlighted that management adhere well to a 'what you put in is what you get' work style.

Debenhams staff stated that they found it encouraging to work to a place of work where you could socialise outside of work and are respected for the effort you put in. Managers were reported as being open and honest and very affable when it came to suggestions.

Harrods, John Lewis, Morrisons, Primark, Tesco, Selfridges… the list is long of retailers who are quoted as being great places to work (there will be exceptions to the rule, of course, but to generalise in the same vein that we know there are inspired areas and staff within the health sector).

So, why has the NHS developed such a bad reputation for supporting its employees?

The same satisfaction website has comments regarding employment in the NHS along the lines of long hours and uncaring management, poor management, undervalued, no support, no teamwork, poor working atmosphere, it's just like you read in the papers, ruled by finance, incompetent managers, abusive treatment… on and on it goes.

Granted this is simply a snapshot of both work places and not representative of every experience, but it provides some interesting insight as to current perceptions and thoughts on employment in the health service.

However, the key theme threaded throughout the above and earlier in the book is that of management.

Though they cannot be held entirely to blame for the current culture of bullying, there are many theories to suggest that, if indeed managers or individuals are promoted to positions of seniority, then it may not necessarily be for the right reasons.

Scott Adams, creator of the comic character 'Dilbert', developed a fascinating theory that, upon closer inspection, does have a great deal of credibility.

He called it the 'Dilbert Principle' (also known as the 'Peter principle') and the basic premise is this - ineffective workers are systematically moved to the place where they can do the least damage; management.

A further definition by Laurence J. Peter and Raymond Hull is that in a hierarchy, every employee tends to rise to his level of incompetence.

Baker, Jensen and Murphy (1988) went further, stating that promotions are used as the primary incentive device in most organisations… which is puzzling because promotion-based incentive schemes have many disadvantages and few advantages relative to bonus-based incentive schemes.

We all know someone, NHS or otherwise, who has been promoted to a more senior position and you think to yourself, "What the (insert expletive here) !"

This challenges one's understanding of the reasons why such a thing would be done.

Why acknowledge that someone is, for example, a bully and then promote them? You are effectively handing them free reign to, potentially, use that power for less than noble intent.

Is such a thing done because there is fear that to not promote them might bring about an employment claim with financial repercussions?

Is it because the individual has friends of family members in high places?

It is because they follow the same trope and behaviour patterns of those higher up in an organisation and, by doing so, they 'fit in' with the sensibility that is being promoted by a chief executive?

Why punish whistleblowers, despite promises in policies that they will be protected, while protecting those who are behaving unprofessionally and in a potentially harmful manner?

References

Baker, George P, Jensen, Michael C and Murphy, Kevin J (1988). Compensation and Incentives: Practice Vs Theory. *The Journal of Finance.* 43: (3) 593-616

Fairburn, J. A., & Malcomson, J. M. (2001). "Performance, promotion, and the peter principle". *Review of Economic Studies* **68**: 45-66.

SARAH, RACHEL AND JESSICA'S STORY

NHS EMPLOYEES

I myself have been qualified for 26 years, with two of my colleagues (for the purpose of this reflection, they shall be known as Rachel and Jessica) implicated having been employed for 27 years and 9 years respectively in the NHS.

I arrived as a staff nurse in 2010 on the ward where I was immediately advised to avoid specific members of staff due to certain perceptions of them; in this case Rachel as I was told the manager did not like her and Jessica as she was, and I quote, 'lazy'.

In my experience with them I early on realised that such suggestions concerning their behaviour where unfounded - I found them both to be hard working, friendly and supportive.

It became clear in a short space of time that career progression on the ward where we worked was dependent on friendships within the division.

Individual persecution for Rachel became so bad that she had to attend counselling.

Though more specific incidences are difficult to discuss due to their nature, I began to realise that there was a particular pattern of behaviour concerning how certain staff were treated - behaviour that involved bullying, intimidation and deliberate exclusion.

A few other examples involve my -

- being asked to revise a piece of reflection. When it was presented to me, I noted it had been revised with the compromising element concerning my manager omitted.
- Being advised not to submit any formal complaints concerning a newly appointed member of staff if anything were to go wrong as they were just 'finding their feet.'

Working in this organisation has left all three of us emotionally exhausted, with high anxiety levels and depressive episodes, emotions that have transcended to our families.

Our goals and aspirations have been ignored and we feel - I feel - that I have missed learning opportunities and the freedom to excel in a a job that I love.

All the experiences that myself and my

colleagues endured have just left us profoundly sad about how one person can make you feel so undervalued.

SIX

'I FEEL I HAVE LET HIM DOWN BY NOT
CONTACTING HIM DURING HIS SUSPENSION. HE
WILL NEVER FORGIVE ME. WHEN I HAD PROBLEMS
WITH ANOTHER STAFF MEMBER, HE HAD BEEN
EXTREMELY SUPPORTIVE TO ME WHICH LED TO
HIM BEING DISCIPLINED. WHEN IT COMES TO HIS
MENTAL HEALTH PROBLEMS, I THINK THE TRUST
HAS PLACED HIM IN A VULNERABLE POSITION."

Choice Theory was developed by Dr William Glasser
in the 1950s and 1960s and has ten axioms -

1. The only person whose behaviour we can
   control is our own
2. All we can give another person is
   information
3. All long-lasting psychological problems are
   relationship problems
4. The problem relationship is always part of
   our present life
5. What happened in the past has everything
   to do with what we are today, but we can
   only satisfy our basic needs right now and

plan to continue satisfying them in the future

6. We can only satisfy our needs by satisfying the pictures in our Quality World
7. All we do is behave
8. All behaviour is Total Behaviour and is made up of four components: acting, thinking, feeling and physiology
9. All Total Behaviour is chosen, but we only have direct control over the acting and thinking components. We can only control our feeling and physiology indirectly through how we choose to act and think
10. All Total Behaviour is designated by verbs and named by the part that is the most recognisable

Though you can adapt many if not all to everyday life, the two that are most relevant when discussing bullying and harassment are numbers one and two; control of our own behaviour and all we can provide another is information.

Looking at the first axiom, Glasser theorised that behaviour is not separate from choice, in so much as we choose how to behave at any time. Essentially, we cannot control anyone's behaviour but our own.

When applied to the subject of this book, choice theory offers an interesting, if uncomfortable possibility.

Do your experiences, mine and others involve the acknowledgement that someone *chose* to be a bully?

The idea is nauseating, but perhaps it is a little more complex than simply someone getting their kicks from persecuting another.

A 'deep dive' survey conducted by NHS England in 2017 found that more than half of NHS employees had experienced bullying at some point during their career. Free texts comments went further in regards to the 55% of those who said they had experienced bullying, saying that '… it doesn't appear that much is done to tackle the initial rumblings from staff who are experiencing bullying until something catastrophic happens…', 'I think the NHS as a whole believes they act fairly…', 'There was absolutely no acknowledgement to get to the point of lodging a grievance…'

This survey led to NHS England stating it would develop 'Respect at Work Contacts', whose role would be to support and protect staff who raised concerns.

This project was due to launch in September 2017 with roles implemented in 2018.

During my research for this book, I was unable to speak to one NHS organisation who had implemented these roles, with a number not even aware of what it was (most recent statistics state that there are 2300 NHS hospitals in the U.K; I only contacted 12 so it is important to note that this is only 0.5% of NHS hospitals), but I would be very interested to hear from anyone who works in an NHS organisation where this has been implemented and how it is working.

But going back to choice theory, do people and, in this case, nurses, choose to be bullies and/or harass colleagues?

My own experience lead me to believe that, whilst initially the behaviour towards me was clumsy, unskilled, unfair and born of either the unspoken frustrations of my colleague not getting what they wanted from me or them trying to undermine me, I ultimately ended up believing it was more about power; not them trying to abuse me deliberately but more trying to assert their power (or perceived perception of power) over me.

So, what began as an attempt to express unhappiness at my questioning of their behaviour towards junior staff members, ended up being others using my situation as an opportunity to make a name for themselves… at least, that is the view I have reconciled myself with over a period of time.

However, I am acutely aware and acknowledge that, indirectly, my own feelings and behaviour may have contributed to others developing this perspective.

And this is why.

- A good leader should be able to manage their emotions. Realising and ultimately accepting (it took me a while, but that is another story) that I had mental health problems meant that my emotions were often all over the place. I may not have had any outbursts (and none were reported), but I imagine my own struggles with my mental health created ripples that I was unaware of. Behaviour is tangible, however presented, and is interpreted and re-interpreted whether we like it or not. It makes no difference that I try to be an honest, loyal and decent person; any emotions that seeped from me during this time may have had far-reaching repercussions.

- Consistency is something that, by default, you cannot have if there is only one individual you are challenging about their behaviour. If no-one else is expressing bullying tendencies, and your conversations are only ever with the one person who is upsetting others, they will perceive that you are 'picking' on them. You must have standards to work by, but someone takes your questioning of them as inequality, it could be perceived that you are being inconsistent with the standards you yourself set.

- Challenge poor behaviour. The main element to take away is that behaviour should be challenged if inappropriate: general, non-specific commentary in feedback has no place, but seek guidance and support if you are uncertain how to proceed.

Looking at the second axiom, that of all we can provide is information. When it comes to the subject of bullying however, this can be problematic. After all, no one wishes to acknowledge they are a bully any more than a senior manager wishes to acknowledge that it takes place within their sphere of influence.

Yet the press and reports are littered with examples of where individuals have raised concerns about bullying, either towards themselves or others, and have been ostracised, dismissed, ignored and, in a few tragic cases, been pushed to the point of suicide.

If an individual coerced another into committing suicide, you can only imagine their would be legal consequences.

How can we live in a world where there appear to be so few?

References

Workplace Bullying; measures and metrics to use in the NHS. Illing, Thompson, Crampton et al, 2016. *School of Medical Education, Northumbria University.*

DAVID'S STORY

'DAVID WILL NEVER UNDERSTAND WHY WE
HAVEN'T CONTACTED HIM OR GOT IN TOUCH.
LOYALTY IS EXTREMELY IMPORTANT TO HIM.'

Words are powerful things. As an author, myself and my colleagues in the literary world, be it, bloggers, readers or writers, know it all too well. That is how, after all, we connect with you within the pages of the book you are reading. Maybe this book?

We like to think we know the words that will make you laugh, cry, chill you to the bone and make you feel safe and happy.

Yet in the big, wide world, words can be dangerous tools. They can be twisted, misconstrued and altered ever so slightly, so that the meaning becomes completely different to what it once was.

You have read actual, true-life examples of bullying within the NHS that, though anonymous, are no less powerful because of their lack of identifiers.

As a 40 something-old man, the very fact that you utter the words, 'I was bullied' is something that attempts to strip away your masculinity.

It shouldn't, yet you cannot help but feel that way.

I was bullied at school, but that was physical.

I was bullied by my father, but that was psychological.

To put my experiences with bullying into context, when I was in secondary school, I used to be made to eat cigarette butts at the back of the bus.

I say made, really I mean to say I was too frightened to say anything other than, "Okay."

The game was you passed around a cigarette and had to maintain the ash on the end. Whoever it fell off on, had to eat it. Oddly, it always fell off on my turn (taking into account we shouldn't have had cigarettes, but that's a different conversation!).

Doesn't half make you feel sick. And to top it off, they never gave me decent cigarettes; always Regal. Could have at least made me eat Benson and Hedges.

But anyway, one day I was informed that serious allegations of bullying had been made against me.

I must have said 'Excuse me' and 'What' dozens of times!

They wouldn't, of course, tell me who said individuals were, but in the back of my mind, I had a good idea...

After being told I'm suspended, I called Kelly, my wife, to tell her.

She asks why?

I say I have no idea really and tell her what I know.

No one speaks to me for over four months from work; HR representatives do. Friends and colleagues, not a word. You see, they have been told they cannot speak to me under any circumstances or they will be disciplined.

This is right before Christmas. I beg one of my friends to speak to me, not about work, just anything;

television, Christmas programmes, her children... anything, just to hear a friendly voice, even if it is via text.

Nothing.

Except a phone call from HR telling me that I have breached the terms of my suspension and am in trouble for texting a friend. I say I wasn't asking about work; on the contrary, I just wanted to speak about anything else. Doesn't matter - I have broken the rules and am given the Crisis Helpline number with advice that if I need to chat with someone, call them.

I just desperately wanted to know that someone, anyone, cared. I wasn't a bully. I knew I wasn't.

I wasn't, was I?

When I had been a child living in Billingham, I was beaten up virtually every day at St Joseph's Primary School. Well, nearly every day.

I hated school. I cried upon having to go. An older boy (who ended up playing for Leeds United) used to chase me around the field and clobber me when he caught me... which he always did because I was teenie-tiny back then. Severely underweight and goofy, with a bowl haircut (thanks, Mum) and NHS glasses (thanks, Mum).

Have you seen NHS glasses now? They're great!

My father was a horrible man; misogynistic wife beater, drunk and psychological abuser of one of his children (he ignored my little brother). He collected me once, from the bus stop when I was in secondary school. I had severe acne from being about 12 to 30 and looked horrendous. My name wasn't David at school; it was Pizza Face. I forgot I was called David until I was in my twenties and someone reminded me!

My Mum was the only person in the world who

never looked at me as though I was a monster; I only ever saw love in her eyes.

My Dad watched me get off the bus and said, "I'm not walking home with a son who looks like that," and left me, whilst the bus full of children laughed. I only saw him occasionally when he wasn't drunk and that was all he had to say to me.

And that was one of the nicer things he did!

But no, not a peep from a soul and it is now Christmas, where I know only that I have been accused of bullying... after reporting bullying.

Was it a coincidence, or was I just making connections where there were none?

Had I done something and not realised, being a bit dim?

But I was determined not to spoil Christmas for my family, so brave face on and we had a lovely Eve and Day. Special, truly. So much love, it was almost tangible.

Boxing Day came and Kelly was supportive of my going out with my friend to relax and try and take my mind off things.

She knew something. I don't know how, but she did.

She had helped me through my recent, reluctant diagnoses of depression and anxiety and was so wonderful about it all. Guiding me and educating me.

But she somehow knew that when I came in that evening, drunk and melancholic, that I would do it.

She had known I would try and kill myself.

Now, before I get into that silliness on my part and

before anyone gets here first, I need to say that the NHS is a fantastic organisation.

Aneurin Bevan spearheaded not only one of the greatest establishments the U.K has ever seen, but a system of free healthcare for all that remains unequalled in the world.

I have seen inspired surgery carried out, met and cared for hundreds of patients while working on a ward, had hundreds of amazing nurses be part of the periphery of my life and be part of something truly unique.

There is no vocation like it, anywhere in my humble opinion.

But which ever way you choose to cut it, it didn't use to be like this. I don't remember thinking it was like this.

I don't mean the circumstances I'm sharing, I mean the lack of humility, responsibility for staff, the caring and protective nature that used to be an everyday part of your working day.

This is present amongst friends and colleagues of course, not all, but many; from higher up in the echelons of the organisation, where decisions are made without any consideration of the repercussions or consequences, I firmly believe there is a distinct lack of understanding of what constitutes a pleasant working environment. That is only my opinion, granted and many would disagree.

Of course, you didn't always have those calm working days. But even the most horrendous, stressful, traumatic day can be tempered knowing that when you return the next day or perhaps the following, you will feel appreciated, love, protected because of the care you provided and most importantly, supported.

But what, in my experience, the NHS do not truly seem to understand at all, is mental health. Not amongst patients, though that could be better outside of the actual mental health hospitals, but amongst its staff.

According to the Department of Health, in 2014 1,497 nurses at 31 trusts took time off related to stress in the workplace, more than 27% in 2012.

This is multi-factorial and not explicitly related to the bullying culture I am referring to. Increasing pressures, acuity of patients, the life expectancy of patients, reduced funding and provisions, all play a part. As a nurse, the one thing you wish to do is care for others; that is why you choose to do it. When you are unable to do that because of bureaucracy, it becomes a spiral of frustrations, irritations and potential problems in an organisation that relies on its workforce; it's very colleagues, to maintain a coherent and functional service.

But it cannot be denied that bullying plays enough if its part.

It is a silent epidemic that no one wants to talk about or admit, but everyone knows exists in one form or another. It isn't, of course, necessary physical (though that sadly does occur in some circumstances). No, it is far more insidious and capricious nowadays.

Of course, the flip side is that there is a risk bullying will be reported that doesn't constitute bullying and because that word has been used, as discussed earlier, immediately there is a knee-jerk reaction instead of a considered and unbiased process.

When I was 14, I had no real friends. Remember, spotty, geeky child (I used to wear my Batman t-shirts beneath my school shirt, as though having them on and keeping them close would imbue me with some courage or strength. It did neither, but no harm, no foul!). A few children used to speak to me and invite me to chat and meet up with them, but I realised later in life that they were never really invested in me as a person and a friend (which is, of course, fine. That is an individual's prerogative... "No, you MUST be friends with me, 'cause my Mum said!!").

But this one day, I was asked if I wanted to meet a load of them before they went to the youth club. Oh, wow, was I excited! I couldn't believe it. Me, they asked me, to go with them? Fantastic!"

I was told what to wear, specifically, to fit in and raced home after school to tell Mum and to say we had to go to the shops to get these items of clothing.

You can see where this is going, can't you?

So, I turn up at the designated meeting point, beneath the Regent Cinema, in my purple stretchy tracksuit bottoms and my purple hooded top, nice white trainers and thinking I looked excellent... I was the coolest. How great they asked me to join them. I was so chuffed. I finally didn't have to be lonely at school.

I think they maybe stopped laughing at me after about ten minutes. Any sensible child/teenager would have seen what was going to happen. But not David the Stupid, no way.

Doh! Bollocks. Crap. For crying out loud. Bugger and so on and so forth.

Anyway, back to my attempted suicide.

Now, I won't bore you with details of my pathetic,

selfish attempt to take my life. That is all in a blog post on my website. Needless to say that I came in at about 0400, drunk and made my way to the kitchen where I removed a knife, sat on the floor and without pretty much any thought at all, started bringing it viciously across my right wrist.

What happened?

Nothing. You know why?

Kelly had removed all of the sharp knives in her prescient moment earlier that day.

What did I have to say about it, at that very moment?

"Did you get these in Ikea, 'cause they don't cut shit."

Much crying, cuddles, kind, soft words that everything will be okay and that was pretty much it (I'm shortening it for brevity).

Scars on my arms and body - 1

Scars on my wrist - 0

Nil-pwa.

However, though no one was supposed to contact me, two people went out of their way to check I was okay. Two lovely individuals who I got on well with, broke policy to just ask how I was.

I shall never forget it.

Interlude

I have always had nightmares since I was a child. My therapist when I was younger told me they were brought on by classic 'Daddy' issues; night terrors, climbing out of my bedroom windows (they had to be nailed shut!), the whole nine yards.

My first vivid memory of my father was me

holding my Mum's hand whilst she held my baby brother and him throwing a telephone at her, breaking her jaw and severely injuring her face.

My Dad... what a guy!

***

Anyway, sleepless nights, blah, blah, blah and it's Monday.

I'm on my way back from Newcastle with Kelly after meeting a friend to discuss a book idea for the two of us to work on.

Mobile rings. I answer (hands-free, of course) and it's an obsequious gentleman telling me off for having spoken to someone I wasn't supposed to but didn't know that I wasn't supposed to.

Bear in mind this gentleman called Kelly and threatened her that if she tried to contact the office where I worked again to ask what was going on, she would be open to disciplinary action. This stemmed from, on the day I was suspended, I had come home, kissed her and walked back out without really saying a word. She had panicked and called my place of work.

Anyway, the situation remained profoundly sad.

I received a few text messages from people at work who had bumped into members of my workplace and had been asked to pass on their love and that they were thinking of me.

It was truly lovely because they had been told they couldn't speak to me, yet had gone to the effort to have messages passed on.

It told me everything would be okay. Maybe I wasn't universally hated and reviled (not that that had been said, but I'm a self-conscious, paranoid, anxiety-ridden individual. I automatically go to everyone hates me, nobody loves me, I think I should go and eat worms).

Long story short - I am cleared and told I could return to work and arrangements would be made.

I think, aside from my marriage, children being born and meeting George Lucas, it was the happiest moment of my life!

Would it be easy returning to somewhere where you knew people had accused you of something you didn't do and had consistently stated was the case?

No. I was under no illusions.

But I so desperately wanted to be back at work, doing what I loved. I wasn't angry with my accusers, I was just sad.

But everything passes and I would move on eventually, as it rightly couldn't go back to how it was, and it would be over and done with.

No recriminations, all forgotten.

I have a meeting about my return to work the following week. I am terrified, scared and anxious beyond belief. I am asked what support I feel I need; I say that I appreciate that my colleagues may need it more, but that I am thankful it is all over and just want to be back at work.

I can come back the following week, the staff will be told, and we say our goodbyes.

All that week, I am so scared. I haven't spoken to anyone for six months. It will be awkward, strange, terrifying, humbling and so much more.

I'm so glad it's over, and my name is cleared. I

knew I wasn't a bully, but it means so much when a panel of your peers agree and support all the evidence you presented to prove otherwise.

The day before my big return arrives and I'm informed I can't return to work.

I'll be honest - I was nearly in tears. I am renowned for having difficulty expressing emotions, both towards others and my own. I don't understand how they are supposed to work. I find them very confusing. But I was more heartbroken than when initially suspended I think. I thought it was done and dusted. Bridges to build, friendships lost, but professionalism remains and most likely, I would move on, but it was done and dusted.

Interlude -

I had been disciplined once before, many years ago. I had confronted a colleague from my place of work about her behaviour towards a senior member of staff and a friend. She had been swearing at her, being disrespectful and made her cry at work.

Everyone I was working with that day saw what was happening, was leaning in to listen to her abusive tirade against my colleague and there's... and did absolutely nothing.

They just sat there, pretending it wasn't occurring.

I couldn't believe that someone they claimed to care so much about and respect so much could be being verbally abused, right in front of them and they did nothing at all.

That was unacceptable to me, so I confronted said abusive colleague and we had an argument in the office. No bad language was used, but voices were raised, I cannot deny.

I was ultimately given a final written warning for three years because of behaviour unbecoming a senior nurse.

I defended my colleague against a bullying, abusive individual and got a final written warning after being cleared of the allegation because I had been angry when confronting her.

Appropriate? Not professionally. I was wrong to confront her in the office but knew that she was prone to lying and that if I confronted her in private, I would have no witnesses. As it happens, it was those un-reactive witnesses who supported me by saying I hadn't done all the things I was accused of and I was so humbled by their public support for me.

It was moving. Despite my feelings towards their inaction at that moment of abuse, I was simultaneously grateful to have such support for me and what I had done.

I was advised I should have ignored it.

Personally, I would do it the same again.

Interlude ends

On the back of this, Kelly wrote a letter, highlighting her concerns for my mental health, the fact that I had tried to commit suicide because of this whole situation and that she had been treated so rudely when enquiring about me all those months ago.

The response was it was 'brought to my attention alongside a number of character references in order to inform a decision as to whether to proceed to a hearing or not. I didn't feel they changed my decision.'

Character references from all over the hospital - consultants, current colleagues, former colleagues and respected senior members of the organisation - evidence stating who was the bully and union support didn't change the decision.

The final part of the story is that I was given a redeployment timetable where they would try and find me a suitable, alternative position.

I secured one interview but was unsuccessful.

Many posts required clinical skills and this is where I was snookered. You see, I had specialised in a role but was now looking for a new post, a post for which I didn't really have any transferrable skills. No-one's fault, I know. Just the way it was. But a bummer? Definitely!

And so, we come full circle, and back to the beginning where I was made unemployed.

I promised myself that if it took me the next day, the next week, the next year, the next 500 years, I would not stop until I revealed the truth and exposed the culture that now exists in the NHS - one of bullying and harassment.

Remember I said the NHS is an inspired organisation and the noblest occupations. I am proud to have contributed even a tiny part to a patient's well being and recovery, whether directly or by tertiary means.

So much good will, amazing care and exceptional procedures take place, every day. That is undeniable and irrefutable.

But there is no argument, supported by the hundreds of articles and documents on the subject, whether by Lord Darzi or Sir Robert Francis or Jeremy Hunt or countless others, that a culture of bullying represents a clear and present danger to the mental health and career wellbeing of some nursing staff, current and in the future, across parts of the NHS.

It must be stopped. And if my words can encourage one more nurse to stand up and say "NO", then I have done something to facilitate a change. And that is all it takes, just one person. Because then you get another, and another, and another, and before long you reach a tipping point, where it carries on under its own inertia.

I learnt so much from my experience. I learnt who, out of my colleagues, truly cared for and would stand by me, throughout everything. I learnt they are the best example of what humanity has to offer and I am forever in their debt. They know who they are. The list is long, but it exists and I am humbled that they cared and believed in me so much that they never faltered in their belief. I was truly moved and didn't realise how many friends I had.

Their words meant so much and shall forever have a place in my heart.

I loved and will always be privileged that I can say I had an 18-year nursing career. I loved every minute of you. You taught me so much. I made plenty of mistakes, but always tried to own up to them. Most importantly, you gave me the opportunity to meet some amazing people - patients and colleagues - who always reminded you that there is so much suffering that can be eased with a smile and so much that can be done when you work together as a team and believe in what it is you do.

And I have to mention my beautiful Turtle.

Kelly never once left my side and literally kept me alive. I put her through so much, inadvertently, but she never gave up on me. She is my sun, moon and stars and never was there a stronger person.

To paraphrase a great man, I shall never forget this. Not one line. Not one day.

I shall always remember when David McCaffrey, the nurse, was me.

(A MORE DETAILED VERSION OF THIS REFLECTION IS AVAILABLE AT https://goo.gl/HAJWU2)

CHAPTER 7 - EVERYONE'S STORY

NHS EMPLOYEES

These are just a few of the messages I have been sent since sharing the concept of this book.

I have hundreds more.

It requires no pre-amble from me.

They speak for themselves.

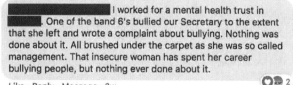

███████████████ I worked for a mental health trust in
██████. One of the band 6's bullied our Secretary to the extent that she left and wrote a complaint about bullying. Nothing was done about it. All brushed under the carpet as she was so called management. That insecure woman has spent her career bullying people, but nothing ever done about it.

Like · Reply · Message · 2w

↳ 1 Reply

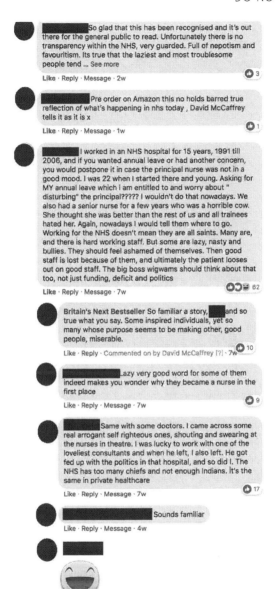

So glad that this has been recognised and it's out there for the general public to read. Unfortunately there is no transparency within the NHS, very guarded. Full of nepotism and favouritism. Its true that the laziest and most troublesome people tend ... See more

Like · Reply · Message · 2w

Pre order on Amazon this no holds barred true reflection of what's happening in nhs today , David McCaffrey tells it as it is x

Like · Reply · Message · 1w

I worked in an NHS hospital for 15 years, 1991 till 2006, and if you wanted annual leave or had another concern, you would postpone it in case the principal nurse was not in a good mood. I was 22 when I started there and young. Asking for MY annual leave which i am entitled to and worry about " disturbing" the principal????? I wouldn't do that nowadays. We also had a senior nurse for a few years who was a horrible cow. She thought she was better than the rest of us and all trainees hated her. Again, nowadays I would tell them where to go. Working for the NHS doesn't mean they are all saints. Many are, and there is hard working staff. But some are lazy, nasty and bullies. They should feel ashamed of themselves. Then good staff is lost because of them, and ultimately the patient looses out on good staff. The big boss wigwams should think about that too, not just funding, deficit and politics

Like · Reply · Message · 7w

Britain's Next Bestseller So familiar a story, and so true what you say. Some inspired individuals, yet so many whose purpose seems to be making other, good people, miserable.

Like · Reply · Commented on by David McCaffrey [?] · 7w

azy very good word for some of them indeed makes you wonder why they became a nurse in the first place

Like · Reply · Message · 7w

Same with some doctors. I came across some real arrogant self righteous ones, shouting and swearing at the nurses in theatre. I was lucky to work with one of the loveliest consultants and when he left, I also left. He got fed up with the politics in that hospital, and so did I. The NHS has too many chiefs and not enough Indians. It's the same in private healthcare

Like · Reply · Message · 7w

Sounds familiar

Like · Reply · Message · 4w

Like · Reply · Message · 4w

Ai dreptate lucrez in spital oxford,azi manegera spune,,pacientul este important"" ce?

Like · Reply · See translation · Message · 4w

89

Like · Reply · See translation · Message · 4w

███████████ sadly the NHS is nowadays a business, like any other. The patient must be the focus, but that is not the case anymore. It's all about how much money can be saved. But as everywhere, there is a lot of dead wood. Too many managers, not enough nurses, and doctors cannot operate on patients because wards are full, new wards cannot be opened as care is too much money. When I was young, you would be in hospital for at least a week after having your appendix out, today you are lucky to stay 8 hours. Very sad

Like · Reply · Message · 4w   👍1

███████████Liliana Ilisei nu numai pacientul e important ci si asistenții. Sau pacienții sunt protejați si au drepturi. Dar personalul? Si noi asistenții trebuie să fie protejați si sa avem drepturi. Vai de tara asta, Anglia. Nu de tara in sine, cat de oameni care trăiesc în ea.

Like · Reply · See translation · Message · 2w

███████████ I was,nt alliwed to choose my annual leave, the rest of the staff chose theirs and the sister would go through after and say, right, you can have that week, that week and that week, with the spaces left.

Like · Reply · Message · 2d

███████████ I have total sympathy

Like · Reply · Message · 2d

Write a reply...   😊 📷 GIF 🎁

███████████ All too often staff who complain in the NHS are told they are being paranoid. Bullies are often promoted and then flaunt their promotion to the ones they have bullied. And if you are clerical and they are clinical you are supposed to bow and scrape b... See more

Like · Reply · Message · 4w · Edited   👍❤️😮 15

↳ View previous replies

Britain's Next Bestseller ███████████ that's my plan. Though they will dismiss it as nonsense, I intended to do everything I can to get it to them all.

Like · Reply · Commented on by David McCaffrey [?] · 4w   👍2

↳ View more replies

███████████ It's so prevelent in the NHS. There are some nasty manipulative individuals who think they are gods and get away with bullying because of their status.

Like · Reply · Message · 5w   👍20

███████████ I had an absolutely fab job with the NHS won national awards for our work. Suddenly new staff joined and it became very different. Whispering/ disclusion/ job I was doing was not good enough (It was just wanted me out). It was so bad took time of sick ... See more

Like · Reply · Message · 4w   👍17

███████████ I don't work in the nhs myself but a lot of my neighbours do. Unfortunately due to bullying in the nhs I had to witness my neighbours body been taken away after she hung herself due to bullying at ███████████ She was a ju... See more

Like · Reply · Message · 1w   😢❤️😮 12

I hope the book takes into account the effect of inordinately high levels of stress due to staff shortages. I am not condoning bullying, I have been bullied but I also know I have not always been as caring and considerate to colleagues and patients as I should be. Ultimately this lead to me leaving nursing. The stress made me unable to to the job as I knew I should.

Like · Reply · Message · 2w 　　　　　　　　　　　 👍 9

↳ 2 Replies

So sad that bullying occurs in the workplace....the bully leaves work at the end of the day and goes home without a second thought about the distress they have caused to their 'victim'
The 'victim' leaves work and takes home the negativity, is unable t... See more

Like · Reply · Message · 3w 　　　　　　　　　　　 👍💬 7

↳ 3 Replies · 5 hrs

people who have experienced this first hand should have their voices heard, its a huge cover up. Its bigger than anyone could imagine.

Like · Reply · Message · 4w 　　　　　　　　　　　 👍 9

↳ 2 Replies

Ive witnessed it and experienced it first hand! At a 'highly acclaimed' uk hospital. What normally happens is the bully is often not great clinically anyway so gets promoted higher up away from direct patient contact! So many times ive seen this happe... See more

Like · Reply · Message · 5w 　　　　　　　　　　　 👍 7

↳ 2 Replies

Managed 43 years of life happy and confident, 1 year into nursing I was on anti depressents. I was lucky the person was promoted (shocker!) And I was back to work and off the tablets. Is it the mainly female environment that creates the bitchiness?

Like · Reply · Message · 2w 　　　　　　　　　　　 👍 4

I was bullied as a student midwife! It left me absolutely floored and stripped me of my confidence and self esteem! Thing is at the time people were too scared to stand up for me as they would have been the next target! I left the course after 3 1/2 Years of rough study for nothing 😢

Like · Reply · Message · 2w 　　　　　　　　　　　 😢👍 5

I was told it was illegal for me to have a witness in the interogation room, illegal for me to speak about it, they had their own legal system that wss beyond reproach and they have the best legal team in the world, they did,nt have to obey any laws as... See more

Like · Reply · Message · 2w 　　　　　　　　　　　 👍 4

I was harrassed by phone, i was rdered to meetings with no union support , infact the union woman slammed the office door in my face.i was constantly sent threatening letters saying i had ignired letters fir appointment,s. Those letters never existed. ... See more

Like · Reply · Message · 1w 　　　　　　　　　　　 😢 2

↳ 9 Replies

91

I find it so sad that bullying is so prevalent in the NHS that there is now a book about it. I'm entering my 20th year in the NHS now, and I'm lucky to have only been subjected to bullying on a very short term basis and only on a couple of occasions. But when it has happened, it has made life unbearable.

I believe one of the reason it persists is a culture of poor people management in so many trusts. I've worked in some trusts that are so incredibly badly run.

Poor and lazy staff are never dealt with, those who do work hard are taken for granted and dumped on by the lazy ones. The decent people who stand up for patients are bullied and/or hounded into leaving. In such organisations patients are never the priority, and I don't understand that. Maybe if there was a strong culture of 'patient first' we wouldn't have these problems. I can't believe that's even up for discussion.

I wonder whether the traditionally low pay of the NHS puts good managers off; maybe they would be better rewarded in the private sector? Just a theory.

I really hope things change soon but I'm not hopeful. I don't think I'll finish my 20th year.

Like · Reply · Message · 1w

Sometimes staff can play the bullying card to get their own way or to try and cover up serious mistakes. Luckily we have a thorough policy in our organisation. I've been on both sides and it's tough. X

Like · Reply · Message · 4w

↳ 1 Reply

Sadly it is condoned. The bullies are ignored or promoted by the senior management . The deputy head of nursing had an office on my ward for 2 years. For 2 years she heard the shouting, the abuse, the belittling and all she did was go to the kitchen, m... See more

Like · Reply · Message · 1w

I have just left a dept where I loved my staff and my role for this reason. Had a horrendous 6 months and couldn't face the fight. It's hard to keep your head above water when ur singled out and for no reason other than organisational merger so they wanted their own staff in. Makes me so sad but u can't fight the powers that be

Like · Reply · Message · 1w

↳ 2 Replies

When you take a stand against it you are on your own .Whistleblowing is the right thing to do but the people who ignore it or condone are promoted and rewarded . Lack of integrity within the NHS management but I have so much respect for the Doctors ,Nurses and Therapists who care and make a difference.

Like · Reply · Message · 1w

You know you are bullied when the B7 does the Christmas and New Year off duty and puts you on 6 nights. Gives everyone else time owing or some annual leave. When you question it she said "do you expect me to change all the off duty now then?" At the time I was married and my husband worked shifts too. The only one whose husband did. Hence I left for a Mon to Fri job and never looked back.

Like · Reply · Message · 4w · Edited

It's seems to be what the NHS was built on. Also gaslighted into thinking you are weak for not coping with it! I manage my life in the NHS by moving around a lot, temporary contracts have become my best friend.

Like · Reply · Message · 3w

I have seen staff bully patients, bully other colleagues , took it to higher management. Continuously brought it to their attention that there was a bullying environment in the ward ! I finally put my notice in when another incident happened with a pat... See more

Like · Reply · Message · 2w

Please investigate the suicide of Anaesthetist, Dr Bundock in the Heath Hospital, Cardiff as her tormentor has been 'cleared by an internal investigation'. I was put through 4 years of hell by my own boss in ▇▇▇▇▇▇▇ but my tribunal win was the only thing that stopped me from ending like her. The despair she must have felt to take her own life whilst in work is difficult to even imagine

Like · Reply · Message · 1w

↳ 2 Replies

Does NHS really care about going on on the frontline? Ever wonder why theyre losing lots of moneydue to rapid turnover of staffing. There are loads of nurses who left NHS due to abuse. Why dont they ask these peoplethe bottomline problem.

Like · Reply · Message · 3d

All too familiar .I spent my working life in the NHS .The unit I worked in closed.I was redeployed.The manager bullied me for several years.I kept a record of what happened.When I complained I was "dismissed".I complained about that manager also.Nothing happened .I simply walked out as it was affecting my health

Like · Reply · Message · 4w

But why is this allowed? Why is the perpetrator protected? I ask because if it was in civilian life ie domestic violence schools etc the ensure the perpetrator is punished. Baffles me why they have their own rules !!!

Like · Reply · Message · 2w

↳ 2 Replies

It happens in private nursing sector too. I reported phyical abuse and restraint of an elderly frail person and after that i was bullied and hounded out of my job. The owners made their deputy manager pick at me at every oppotunity she got. I ended up ... See more

Like · Reply · Message · 1w

I work in the NHS and sadly this is not a shock to me!!! Too many chiefs, not enough indians...rife for bullying!!! Like being back at school....😔

Like · Reply · Message · 3d

Anti bullying policies are worthless. Bullies get more protection than the victims and it will NEVER be wiped out. Bullies win, every time.

Like · Reply · Message · 3w

↳ 1 Reply

I have seen many a good person destroyed by the actions and behaviour of others, myself included and been too afraid to speak out because of the consequences someone once said it would be like committing professional suicide to speak out

Like · Reply · Message · 1d

There wouldn't be bullying if there wasn't so much pressure put on from above . The domino effect means it starts at the top and works its way down to the bottom , each one bullying the one below.

Like · Reply · Message · 3w

There is a whistle blowing policy and staff need to utilise this if they feel three need. Bullying and harassment is wrong and can lead to constructive dismissal!

Like · Reply · Message · 2d

I have ptsd, i still suffer night terrors occasionally , i have fibromyelgia and im convinced its from the trauma i went through.

Like · Reply · Message · 1w

Not only the nhs bullies thrive in most places because people become to psychologically damaged to stand up to them!

Like · Reply · Message · 1w

Nice one, David! I'm looking forward to reading it. I'd love to write a book about the patient bullying too. Best wishes.

Like · Reply · Message · 4w

↳ 1 Reply

They have a system in the prison service which I managed called Professional standards.
It was a vehicle to report wrongdoing in which the Source was always protected.
It would be ideal for the NHS as only the sytem manager knew where the information had come from.
It would give staff the confidence to report wrongdoing without fear .

Like · Reply · Message · 3w

The NHS is a bullies playground! Management encourages it!

Like · Reply · Message · 5w   14

Bullying seems rife in the public sector - NHS, education, councils.

Like · Reply · Message · 5w   6

When I was bullied I was told after the grievance it was a probable breakdown of communication which left me off sick for a long period of time , the bullies remained and I went to another hospital until I took redundancy. Then I got a gagging order !! It's a joke and they let bullies rule in the NHS despite lots of complaints about the bullies . They choose not to rock the boat

Like · Reply · Message · 6w   5

These issues need awareness, it's on going issue within employment all together.

Like · Reply · Message · 6w · Edited   1

It's not only in the clinical area that bullying goes on

Like · Reply · Message · 1w

Bullies should be euthanized! They ruin everything.

Like · Reply · Message · 7w   3

Like · Reply · Message · 3w

In Wales we still have community health councils, whose officers will intervene on a patient's behalf to address issues such as bullying. Is it not the role of unions to assist with such matters ? If they are failing to act then withdraw - very noisily - from membership.

Like · Reply · Message · 1w

You are powerless and are isolated and moved on if a powerful Consultant is the bully you really have no chance unless you have the strength and money to take to a civil court

Like · Reply · Message · 1w

And into essex... even the Drs do it.... no help from Hr or managers

Like · Reply · Message · 4w

Ordered it on my kindle. Hope it's a best seller David

Like · Reply · Message · 5w

None of these bullies want to hear they have been intercepted. If you let them know they will make your life hell, following you, checking up on you, harass you, micro manage you etc. They hide behind policies and sop's. They are psychopaths , narcissi... See more

Like · Reply · Message · 1w   3

Britain's Next Bestseller   you raise some very interesting points. There is definately an element of sociopathy in the sense that, they are devoid, or seem to be, of emotion in regards to the harm they cause. I am uncertain if they don't realise or just dont care, but what you say about hiding begins regulations and seniority is very true

Like · Reply · Commented on by David McCaffrey [?] · 1w   5

Rings so true   3

Like · Reply · Message · 7w

It's not exclusive to the NHS .. it's everywhere   2

Like · Reply · Message · 1w

Could write a book as well

Like · Reply · Message · 2d

How very sadly true

Like · Reply · Message · 4d

Very interesting read!!!!

Like · Reply · Message · 6w

Can't wait to read it David . Pre ordered. Xx

Like · Reply · Message · 7h

read the comments on here

Like · Reply · Message · 4w

Just like in most work places

Like · Reply · Message · 3w

↳ 2 Replies

What you Emma never

Like · Reply · Message · 6w

Read your policy, I did and used it in an email against my bully (the policy says to open dialogue if possible) so I emailed how I felt and said I want it to stop. It did, for me 😔 unfortunately I can't fight every one else's battle, I've tried in the past only to be met with a denial 😔 then I'm the bad guy. But read your policies, it's a start. Nursing took its lead from the armed forces, hence the bullying 😔😔 Who cares for the carers? 😔

Like · Reply · Message · 3w

Part of the problem is is zero or very poor training to be a Team Leader/ Manager etc.
30 years ago I did half an MBA and we covered all aspects of managing your team to get the best for them and from them. These last 20 years I have worked as a lowly... See more

Like · Reply · Message · 3w

Why just now.. This been going on for many long years. Its a common scenario at NHS hospital that staff members were bullied and harassed if not by patients or relatives/families of patients or higher ranking colleagues

Like · Reply · Message · 5d

One thing i dud discover and know for a fact, we really do have souls, or spirits, because i felt mine dying, i could feel its pain, if i had ever doubted our spiritual bodies, the experience showed me beyond proof, we all have a soul, spirit or whatever you want to call it.

Like · Reply · Message · 2d

I had 6 weeks of stress leave at the end of last year because of harassment in the workplace. I'm a secretary. I stand up to the management now.

Like · Reply · Message · 3w

↳ 1 Reply

I could write a book about the bad practices, things I had to do, consultants who bullied me as well as finding fraudulent claims but as I said I've a gagging order but I will write that book it was a right den of iniquity, why would you put a gagging order on someone if you have nothing to hide!!!

Like · Reply · Message · 4d

I got bullied by a narc at   , reported her .... And nothing was done . I no longer work for the NHS , and if I see her on the street .... Well she'll learn

Like · Reply · Message · 1w

Don't know what is wrong with the system. Have people forgotten why they joined nursing...to actually help people and that includes colleagues. It's so sad to hear people's stories of having to leave their profession through lack of support and bullying. Exposure is key...everyone has rights.

Like · Reply · Message · 2d

It seems, do no harm to the patients they look after, but that doesn't apply to in how they treat their staff (some staff members not all)

Like · Reply · Message · 3w

I suffered bad depression. It's one rule for one and one for another . Hate how they lie belittle I have many insidents .

Like · Reply · Message · 1w

GABRIELLA'S STORY

FORMER NHS EMPLOYEE

As a staff nurse I recall a number of incidents where I look back now and realise I was being bullied, but didn't acknowledge it at the time. All concern consultants, but one that particularly sticks in my mind was regarding a wound dressing not having been taken down prior to a ward round.

I had only been made aware moments before the consultant turned up, so it hadn't yet been done. He was so angry, he poked me in the shoulder repeatedly, hard enough to leave a bruise.

When I raised it to my manager at the time, I was told that they can simply 'do what they want' and that was the end of it.

On another occasion a consultant, whom I was unaware was a consultant as his patient was a sleep out from another ward, made an unannounced visit. As we are taught to do when unfamiliar with someone visiting, I asked who he was.

The consultant immediately became angry, so much so that his patient actually had to intervene to calm him down. Once again, I reported this behaviour to my manager only to be told that is 'how they are'.

Again, no action was taken.

A third occasion concerned a staff-grade doctor who I was friendly with and who everyone got on well with. On this occasion, I was alerted to the fact there was an urgent phone call from theatre regarding a patient's blood results.

Slightly apprehensive, I took the call only to realise from the voice who it was and responded with, "It's only you."

He lost his temper, hung up the phone and made his way to the ward, waving his briefcase in my face and asking who did I think I was saying it was 'only him' on the phone.

I tried to explain that it was simply an affectionate way of saying I was relieved it wasn't one of the doctors with an intimidating reputation, but this did little to calm him down.

He did later apologise, but really the damage had been done by then.

There is a fine line between having respect for someone and being terrified.

I know of other occasions where issues

concerning consultants and their behaviour have been raised by staff nurses to managers, some with supporting evidence, but all have been advised not to pursue it as it would be damaging to the nurse's reputation.

AFTERWORD

There is no right answer, no magic wand that can answer the questions posed nor solve the problem of bullying, not just within the NHS but in other businesses and organisations.

I have spoken to many employees within and formerly of the NHS; many do not have stories of bullying, personally or otherwise.

But as you have read, many, too many, do.

My word isn't the final word on the subject.

The Ben Cohen Stand Up Foundation, founded in 2011 was the world's first foundation dedicated to raising awareness of the long-term, damaging effects of bulling.

Ditch the Label was founded by Liam Hackett in 2006. Based on his personal experiences, his charity is one of the few digital, anti-bullying charities.

Bullying UK was formed in 2010 on the back of Family Lives and offers somewhere were individuals can be listened to and supported in a non-judgemental environment.

Kidscape is somewhere that strives for all children to grow up in a world free from bullying.

Anti-Bullying Alliance, BulliesOut, Cybersmile, Stamp It Out, Let's Remove It campaign... there are so many. The very fact that so many exist should be enough to make us all pause for a moment and consider *why* they need to exist in such quantities.

A link between bullying in the NHS has been made clear, a fact supported by the aforementioned Let's Remove It campaign. I have heard said that bullying amongst staff, particular nurses, in the NHS is not within the gift of the NMC to address as it doesn't affect patient safety. Let's Remove It believes that the extent of bullying and undermining throughout healthcare is well documented, with surgery often being reported as being a speciality where it is particularly prevalent (raced.ac.uk; accessed 16/10/2018).

Their longline is 'Bullying harms your profession and patients. Let's remove it.'

What you have read are the personal experiences of genuine NHS employees.

The chapters interspersed with the reflective recol-lections are my own opinion. Despite the heart-breaking end to my nursing career, I have to be honest in saying that the experience opened up so many other opportunities and avenues for me I would have never considered.

I guess not having a secure employment future meant that, without that as a safety net, I took leaps of faith I wouldn't have ordinarily entertained.

I got to spend more time with my children and Kelly.

I got the opportunity to try my hand at being a radio broadcaster.

I got to spend more time writing.

I was able to, after some time, go back to nursing with some fantastic individuals.

And, perhaps most tellingly, I found myself being invited to attend the Ben Cohen Stand Up Foundation Inaugural Conference to speak about my experiences with workplace bullying, surrounded by many gifted and experienced individuals. It is indeed humbling to know that others are interested in hearing your voice, but even more humbling to be given an opportunity to speak for others and direct awareness of the issues that bullying in the NHS raise.

I wanted to do something that could perhaps help others; see if I could use my experience to highlight the suffering of others within and without the NHS.

I cannot say that I will make a difference, but I can state unequivocally that I will never stop trying.

It's the least I can do after all the support others showed me.

My father never once told me he was proud of me. But maybe, by trying to help others, in even this small way, by showing others that if you speak up you will be heard and people will be there for you, to catch and support you, I can make Liam, Jakey, Cole, Kelly, John, Alan, Fiona and my Mum proud.

Someone told me a story about their sister committing suicide because of bullying in the NHS. Even worse (if it even could be) is that the sister had to continue to attend work for the very same organisation that had been instrumental in damaging her sister's mental state in the first place.

How horrific an experience.

How terrible a fact.
How important a cause.

References

https://www.rcsed.ac.uk/news-public-affairs/news/2017/june/bullying-and-undermining-campaign-let-s-remove-it (accessed 16/10/2018)

ACKNOWLEDGMENTS

There are too many individuals to thank for their help with this book - good and bad.

Those who were supportive and remained by my side know who they are.

Those who didn't know who they are also.

Without all, I wouldn't have had this opportunity.

So, to all, I simply say thank you.

USEFUL CONTACTS

Ben Cohen Stand Up Foundation - http://www.standupfoundation-uk.org

Ditch the Label - https://www.ditchthelabel.org

Bullying UK - https://www.bullying.co.uk

Kidscape - https://www.kidscape.org.uk

Anti-Bullying Alliance - https://www.anti-bullyingalliance.org.uk

BulliesOut - https://bulliesout.com

Cybersmile - https://www.cybersmile.org

Stamp It Out - http://www.stamp-it-out.co.uk/

Let's Remove It - https://www.rcsed.ac.uk/news-public-affairs/news/2017/june/bullying-and-undermining-campaign-let-s-remove-it

MIND - https://www.mind.org.uk

Samaritans - https://www.samaritans.org

Childline - https://www.childline.org.uk

11858768R00072

Printed in Great Britain
by Amazon